CHOOSE HIM

How to Get Clear, Define What You Want,
and Attract The Man of Your Dreams

DEB GARRAWAY

Copyright © 2010 by Deb Garraway

Published and distributed in the United States by: Brilliance MultiMedia, Alamo, California: www.debgarraway.com

All rights reserved. No part of this book may be reproduced by any mechanical, photographic, or electronic process, or in the form of a phonographic recording; nor may it be stored in a retrieval system, transmitted, or otherwise be copied for public or private use – other than for "fair use" as brief quotations embodied in articles and reviews – without prior written permission of the publisher.

The author is grateful for permission to use the following copyrighted materials:
Excerpt from article by Martha Beck "Go Tell Alice," *O Magazine* 2/2008.
Portion of painting "The Muse of Conscious Awakening" by Martina Hoffmann, Boulder, CO.
All interior photos used with permission. © 2010 iStock.

ISBN (10) 0982582218
ISBN (13) 9780982582213

Disclaimer

All information contained within this book exists for the sole purpose of general education and self-realization. The ideas expressed by the author stem from her own experience and her experience with women who have been led through the Choose Him Process. The author does not advocate or endorse using this book as a substitute for therapy or other self-help modalities. The author gives no expressed or implied warranties and assumes no responsibility for individual actions, aspirations, or fulfillment of dreams, though her intention is that readers use this book as a tool to assist them on their life path.

"There is something infinitely richer in the life we choose instead of one we let happen to us."

In loving memory of Cleo and Edwin Garraway.

Contents

Give Yourself Permission to Dream 1

Introduction 3

What's Different About This Book? 9

Part 1. You Get to Choose 11

Part 2. How to Get the Most Out of This Book 18

Part 3. How Did We Get Here? 20

Part 4. The Choose Him Process 34

    Step 1. Reflect—It's All About You 37

    Step 2. Create—Your Dream Man Story Creator 64

    Step 3. Attract—Manifest Your Own Ending 133

Part 5. What To Expect Next 139

Afterword 159

Related Reading 163

Appendix A. Relationship Models 164

Appendix B. U.S. Marital Status 166

Acknowledgments 167

About the Author 168

Give Yourself Permission to Dream...

about your ideal man,
about your relationship with him,
about your life together.

When you start the Choose Him Process, you become the dreamer and author of your authentic life with the man of your dreams. As you journey through this process, you breathe life into that vision that has been too long dormant or locked away.

Here is a glimpse of an excerpt created from the interactive Story Creator template:

> ...What my guy loves about me is my curiosity and positive attitude toward life. He is thoughtful in supporting me in my alone time when I want to tinker in my hobbies, read, or dig in the garden. He appreciates that my spirit is optimistic, adventurous, and upbeat and he loves my laugh and thinks I'm funny.

He's proud that I am very open-minded, confident, and nonjudgmental. When he speaks about me to others, he says that I'm the best thing that ever happened to him, which makes me feel respected, free to be who I am, and unconditionally loved.

My man encourages me to pursue my dreams by helping me with planning and always being positive. It's natural for him to find creative ways to make me feel special. He shows his romantic side by planning special things for us to do together. He's the kind of man who would surprise me with a trip to Morocco and that makes me appreciate his zest for adventure.

When I walk through the door, he makes me feel adored. In our quiet time together, I know he feels appreciated and confident and he always says I add so much to his life. I know for sure that he makes me feel unconditionally loved.

I'm proud that my man is incredibly conscious, respectful, and comfortable in his own skin. . . . When I sit back and watch him, I truly appreciate his grounded, genuine, and down-to-earth way of being. . . .

The Choose Him Process is an opportunity to dream, to allow for what might be possible. You're likely going to be engaging with energy that's atrophied because you've been asleep to it, or actively ignoring it. In these pages, I invite you to allow that energy to be free and to allow yourself to express your heart's desire.

Introduction

"A dream man loves who you are and encourages you to follow your aspirations and dreams."

This book is a product of my life experiences, relationships, and learning over the past forty years. Much to my surprise, the process of writing this book uncovered a profoundly ingrained coping strategy I had formed in childhood as a bi-racial African-American woman. Growing up in the 1950s and 60s, as the daughter of a dark-skinned father and a light-skinned mother, I had to stand by and watch them endure appalling verbal abuse and discrimination throughout their marriage. They not only tolerated the mistreatment, but never complained and silently accepted their plight. I grew up believing that I needed to find a way to avoid the pain of rejection, but more important, to succeed without limitations in a cruel world.

My challenge in coming into my own self-esteem and personal power was compounded by the fact that I look Caucasian and was allowed to pass through doors that my own dark-skinned family and other blacks could not. You see, I was straddling two worlds. Part of me felt guilty for escaping the judgment and limitations imposed on blacks. The other part of me felt shame for being of African-American heritage. Overriding these two dynamics was my determination to be successful and find my place in the world against all odds. I have suppressed these feelings of guilt, shame, and rage (yes, rage!) all my life, and believe it or not, these emotions have only come to surface since I started writing this book. I invite you to the Afterword in this book on page 159 if you feel called to read more about my story.

In my desire to be truly authentic and certain that I'm walking my talk in all I've written in this book, I was obliged to look at my own paradigm prisons. I have found that the power of writing and delving into my deepest motivations has compelled me to peel back even more barriers to my own self-awareness. This experience has evoked revelations that have led me from fear of being who I am to embracing my authentic self and deeper self-acceptance. After decades of talking with women about our concerns, our dreams, and what moves us, I feel confident about the liberation we can experience when we free ourselves from the confinement of old identities and step more into our truth.

Over the past decade, it's been my modus operandi to support and champion women to overcome fear and strive for their dreams. I have long been aware of the importance of the women in my life. I have a remarkable daughter, three wonderful sisters I'm very close to, and my extraordinary mother was a tremendous influence on who I am today. I am also blessed with many brilliant women friends who have journeyed with me on my personal growth path. Whenever I have succeeded in a challenge or experienced a new perspective, I have shared it with other women.

In the early 1970s, I was a twentysomething newlywed attending San Francisco State University. This was one of the first times in my life that I actively sought out like-minded women to talk about women's issues and bettering our circumstances in life. And it wouldn't be the last! I started a small rap group of women, mostly comprised of the wives of my first husband's colleagues. This had nothing to do with the current genre of rap music. We got together to talk about our truths and feelings about our society, spouses, roles, and purpose in life. We were young housewives—many of us young mothers—who would sit on the floor around the living room coffee table into the wee hours of the morning, drinking wine and delving deeply into the meaning of life. Conversation usually centered on what was wrong with our cultural norms and the empty, confused feelings we women were experiencing. We didn't know what to do about our frustrations. Percolating in the background was the fact that the '60s were behind us, and many of us were experiencing the shift in consciousness through the women's movement towards equal rights. It opened our minds to the possibilities of new opportunities and new ways of expression—but we weren't seeing enough of these opportunities and expressions being put into action!

We'd come a long way, baby, but we weren't quite there yet. And we're still not all the way there today.

✳✳✳

Fast-forward two decades to 1994, when I found myself with two divorces behind me, as well as several other disappointing long-term relationships. I was now in my mid-forties, and ready to pursue personal growth work to understand and heal the part of me that believed men defined my self-worth, beauty, and lovability. I was frustrated and fed up that I didn't seem to have any control over this part of my life. I felt as if I was just supposed to wait for the next man to come along and choose me; then I'd try to fit into his world and hope it would all work out. Repetitive frustration prompted me to write out my original vision for what I wanted. I realized that my anger was part of what helped me access the permission I needed to grant myself to ask for what I wanted—not just what I thought might be possible in a future relationship. I was a rebel with a cause for *me*.

In April 1995, at age forty-seven, I wrote out the first version of my Dream Man vision based on probing my heart and my core desires. Little did I know that this original vision would lead me to help many women through the same process in years to come, and would serve as the inspiration for the Dream Man Story Creator and the impetus for the Choose Him Process.

When I wrote out that original Dream Man vision, I decided to do it in the same way I approached my professional achievements. I had pursued career objectives through clearly defined goals and focused intention. I'd read about the Law of Attraction when I was a teenager, and I was impressed by the principle it holds that you can manifest what you want in life with your thoughts and feelings. Since that early time, anytime I wanted something important, I made it happen through writing it out and then imagining what it would feel like to have it already. I would think about it with confident expectation in vivid detail and hold the positive feelings inside me many times a day. I'd done that for absolutely everything I'd ever wanted, from material things to business and life experiences to improving aspects of myself. It finally struck me that I could actually employ that same process for a man. I thought of this man I was envisioning as my Dream Man because, until that time, I truly believed that the type of man and relationship I wanted was a fairytale fantasy—something that could only exist in my dreams. Given my life experience, I innately knew that I couldn't just envision this man solely from my mind or have him manifest after listing the qualities and characteristics I desired. I needed to create a vision of him through the feelings that I wanted to experience with him and in our day-to-day life. I was determined that I would either manifest this man of my dreams, or be content to remain single. Eleven months to the day later I met my Dream Man, and we were married ten months after that.

***

In 2003, after training to become a life coach, I started noticing a common theme among my clients—they were stuck in various belief patterns that were preventing them from truly being open to finding the man of their dreams. As part of my practice, I mentored women to envision and attract the man of their dreams. Hearing women's stories about their relationship experiences and most intimate desires led me to start compiling data in earnest.

Using my original Dream Man vision, which had led me to find and choose my own husband, I started working with women to extract and transcribe their exact words as they divulged their most personal thoughts and desires about what they wanted in a partner and their relationship. Their feedback, along with contributions from my expert consultants, resulted in a unique and in-depth tool—the Dream Man Story Creator—designed to help them write the story of their Dream Man.

During my work as a life coach, I've issued surveys, interviewed over one hundred women, and coached numerous others. My coaching style is what I call a "co-spiritor," in which I connect with my clients' core essence through an intense probing technique. But this process also took a lot of time, and I could only work with a limited number of women. As I started thinking about the possibility of reaching a broader group of women, I realized that creating their own stories was the thing that was connecting them to their sense of what was possible. Writing your vision of what you want actually connects you to the feelings you want to experience with your man and in your life together. It dawned on me that I was witnessing women connecting to their own innate sense of power through their feelings. This is at the core of feminine intuition, which so many of us unconsciously ignore because it's not valued in our society. The idea that it is possible for women to envision what they want and not just find, but choose, a relationship is at the heart of Choose Him. And the Choose Him Process is the very process you'll get to experience and write out for yourself in the pages that follow. The result will be a new vision for attracting the man of your dreams. But first, we'll delve into some common belief systems that have likely kept you stuck or prevented you from getting what you want. It's important to define what these are so that you can move past them and onto creating what you want.

***

Choose Him represents my efforts to advance a shift in women's consciousness that is progressively permeating throughout all arenas of our culture. Women are beginning to recognize that despite our great social and economic progress, we are still subordinating many of our feminine values in deference to masculine qualities and ideals that are deemed to be more powerful. The irony is that while we've been compromising some of our most intuitive and feminine principles in our efforts to obtain some of that power, we continue to hold onto antiquated models of mating roles and romantic partnering. Consider the fact that most relationships don't last, and fifty percent of marriages end in divorce. It's obvious that it's time for a change in our current perceptions and cultural models. Current partnering paradigms are outdated, and we're stuck in a repetitive spin cycle while blaring signals are crying out for updated perspectives. It's time for us to pursue higher ideals and more realistic guidelines and expectations for creating intentional relationships.

This book is a practical tool to help you push through self-imposed boundaries about who you are and what you desire. It's a realistic guide that will support you to embrace the woman you already are and who you are becoming—your potential. Your individual goals and dreams don't end when you meet the right man; it's a new beginning that enriches your own life story, so it's important that he's the kind of man who will support you on that journey. The first step is about waking up and becoming aware of the paradigm prisons we falsely believe we're locked into. The second step is to peel back the layers and expose your authentic self by becoming honest and real about what is true about you and what you truly want, which leads to authentic personal power. The third step is to form enlightened, supportive, and evolving partnerships in which both women and men hold balanced roles, where independence and individuality is honored. For this type of relationship, today's modern woman is looking for what I call a Dream Man.

For some of you, searching for a Dream Man may seem like some retro throwback to Leave-It-To-Beaver land or Stepford wives. First, let me assure you that this process is no such thing. It is, in fact, a very empowering process rooted in the latest research about how our minds work and how we change old patterns into new models that can transform our lives. Dream Man is a universally understood term for the kind of man who not only will meet the majority of your criteria for an ideal mate, but will also fulfill your most intimate desires, needs and dreams. You know, the kinds of wishes and wants that often feel like fantasy, or something you can only dream about.

A Dream Man is not a perfect robot without any flaws. The dream is about fulfilling your desire to find a man who is a partner with you in navigating the ebb and flow of life, and who can walk beside you through the joys and sorrows. He is one who is willing to fully participate with you in authentic partnership. He's not a knight in shining armor who's going to show up to rescue you from your life—we're not interested in promoting the idea of fantasy happily-ever-afters. This process is about what happens in the "ever after." Real life continues after the newness of meeting, lust, and romance. It's about the beginning of the real story: the ways you interact day to day, develop intimacy, communicate, handle conflicts and life's challenges, rejoice in the gifts and the blessings, and fulfill your dreams. All these things comprise the true story that determines whether a relationship is sustainable.

When I talk about the true story or the real story, I'm talking about authenticity. Most of us feel authentic in many areas of our lives. We ask for what we want, know we deserve to have it, and we choose what's compatible for us. So why aren't we exhibiting this same behavior where men are concerned? We don't have to wait to be chosen by a man. This book will guide you to ask for what you truly want and show you how to get it. You'll be surprised at all the things you have never thought of that directly impact the success of a relationship. Choose Him points you in this new direction, showing you how to choose true partnerships that reflect the real story. In a true partnership, neither partner defines the other's identity, nor are they codependent (what you do reflects on me). I wasn't one of those women who found her Dream Man easily. It took me years of coming into my own—two previous marriages and lots and lots of dating the wrong men. My Dream Man, to whom I've now been married for thirteen years, didn't give me my identity. And he certainly doesn't define who I am today. But having my Dream Man has provided me a supportive foundation for unveiling deeper layers of my authenticity, dreams, grace, and my own identity as a woman. My Dream Man fully accepts me for who I am—my authentic self—and supports my aspirations and potential for who I am becoming.

At the center of this work is the simple but profound idea that you choose your Dream Man. Through the Choose Him Process that comprises the majority of this book, you will envision your Dream Man through the lens of your authentic self and receive follow-through tips on how to make him a reality. The message of this book is about starting with yourself—and that's exactly where the Choose Him Process starts: with you getting clear about you.

Choose Him is about awakening women to the things that aren't working anymore. It's a call to action to get out of our old ways of thinking and to attract the man of our dreams by tapping into our power and embracing our feminine attributes, such as intuition, creativity, and receptivity . Once you discover or reclaim your true self, you will be on the path to bringing into your life a man who inspires you to be your very best self. In the following pages, you will be led through a very precise process that details how to get clear, define what you want, and attract your Dream Man. All that's required of you is true presence and commitment to the process, as well as honest assessment of how you've approached dating and relationships in the past and how you would like to approach them moving forward.

What's Different About This Book?

Although the title and subtitle state what this book is about—getting clear, defining what you want, and attracting your dream man—the value of this process hinges on the issue of choice. You get to choose him. What a novel concept! What's unique about this book is the Choose Him Process, a three-step process that's detailed in Part 4. This process is unlike anything you've ever done. The Dream Man Story Creator is much more than a visualization—it's interactive, fun, and freeing, and it encourages you to dream big and manifest what you create. The Choose Him Process is wholly unique, and if you can allow yourself to be open to the whole process and see it through from start to finish, what you'll end up with will change the course of your life. The Choose Him Process is:

- a stirring, rewarding, and fun experience that ends with a detailed, tangible, and vibrant story of your come-to-life Dream Man.
- a process that's designed to:
  - ~ assist you to transform erroneous and limiting beliefs and patterns

- ~ uncover deeper levels of authenticity to reveal what you truly desire in a man
- ~ maximize your radiance and your attraction factor
- a tool to help you understand your old ways of thinking and make space for new ideas, to connect with your feelings, and to ignite attraction from your authentic personal power, feminine intuition, and wisdom.
- a source of inspiration to help you shift limited perceptions and futile dating techniques to help you find more joy and romance in your own life.

Although the Choose Him Process is the key to breaking out of your limiting belief systems and finding—and choosing—the man of your dreams, Parts 1 through 3 are valuable to understanding how you got here and how to best take advantage of what this process has to offer. It's important to orient yourself to the material you're about to get into, so that you understand how truly deep-rooted our patterns about how we think about men really are. My intention with Choose Him is to help you out of your antiquated beliefs and paradigms—those things that are subtly holding you and women everywhere in self-denigrating patterns of social inequality. This book is about a paradigm shift. It's about creating awareness around the evolution of women and men in relationship, leaving old romantic fantasies behind (being swept off your feet to fate and chance), and shifting to intentional partnering through energetic compatibility and what I call magnetic resonance—your energetic echo. By the end of this book you'll not only be equipped with your Dream Man story, but also with useful tips and a shifted perception of your own behaviors that will help you navigate the dating world in an empowered way.

PART 1. *You Get to Choose*

> "You are significant, you are influential, your potential is essential. You are fempotent!"

FROM FRUSTRATION TO FREEDOM

By the time I awakened to the fact that my relationships were not advancing at nearly the same pace as my professional life, I was mad. I wasn't angry with any of my exes, or with men in general. I was perturbed at the paradigm that exists in our culture that tells us that women must be chosen by men, that we must meet what we've been conditioned to believe are male standards of beauty and desirability. Of course, underneath this anger was plenty of sadness, too—that the reality of my situation didn't match with what I'd always believed I could have. I now know that much of that has to do with the cultural expectations set up for young girls around what to believe about love and relationships.

In my interviews with over one hundred women, I found that most women, consciously or not, still cling to an underlying belief that men hold the power to define our beauty and value. They are the ones who govern the customs for dating and decide whether to ask us to marry them. Simply put, we continue to relinquish the power to define our feminine identity to men. And it's not their fault. My expert sources tell me men are confused. It's not that they want all that responsibility, either. In part it's a tradition we don't know how to redefine, and in part it's the media, movies, and cultural norms that continue to endorse and advance the paradigm.

When I finally shed that limiting perspective and began defining who I am and what I want, and declaring that I would accept no less than my ideal man, my entire way of being shifted. I felt a sense of personal power when I gave myself permission to choose my life partner according to my authentic standards and needs. I decided what I wanted. I let go of the mindset that my identity ought to be defined by men and that I needed to be chosen by a man. That concept was truly liberating.

So what about you? Do you identify with any of the following thoughts or experiences?

- I'm smart, attractive, make my own money—I'm a great catch. Why don't I have a man?
- What's wrong with me? Aren't I lovable?
- I'm tired of being alone.
- Who am I and how do I fit in the world without a man?
- I don't want to grow old with no one to love me and share my life.
- I'm tired of drama and just want a real partner and friend to share my life.
- Isn't there a man out there who really understands me?
- Men used to chase me and I had my pick of them; now they don't even see me.
- How am I supposed to be or act around the men I meet?
- I'm so uncomfortable and anxious out there in the dating world.
- Why am I asking for more pain and heartache with a man?
- Trying to find the right man is too much work and disappointment.
- Dating is too hard. I give up.

If you've had such thoughts, you are not alone. The good news is that there's a way through these painful and confusing feelings. There's some work involved, but the end result will be well worth it, and you can do it privately in your own time without a coach or instructor. The Choose Him Process is a personal, intimate, and exciting process that will give you so much more than your Dream Man. It will reacquaint you with your true self, enhance your way of being and feeling about yourself, get you clear about what you want, and give you tools to empower yourself in an authentic way. There are no games to play or phony rules to follow. You get to be you—just more of the real you. I've translated my forty-plus years of mistakes, hard knocks, and painful experiences, along with those of countless other women, into a process that has positively changed my life and their lives—and gotten us what we want.

Instead of our identities being derived from the reflection of men (and what we think they want), we can redefine our identity through our own mirror of authenticity, worthiness, and the truth of what we truly want. I believe women are the quintessential creators and have the power to evolve cultural ideals and expectations for ourselves and our relationships. This begins with individually claiming who we are authentically, what we care about and value, and how we choose to live our lives from a place of self-love and genuine personal power.

DISPELLING THE MYTH

It's important to clear up the myths of scarcity of available men, and that all single women are desperate to find a mate. The U.S. Census Bureau's 2005–2007 Survey reports for the 35–64 age range, there are 1.7 million more men than women who have never married. It is only the 65-plus age range that shows significantly more single women than men, primarily due to women being widowed at four times the rate of men.

To give you the highlights, the following summary shows the statistics for the ratio of single women to single men from the 2005–2007 census. The detailed comparison can be found in Appendix B.

2005–2007 AMERICAN COMMUNITY SURVEY RATIO OF SINGLE WOMEN TO SINGLE MEN		
Age Range	Single Women	Single Men
20–34	9	11
35–44	8	8
45–54	8	7
55–64	3	2
65+	3	1

Add to these statistics the numerous studies conducted by experts such as sociologist E. Kay Trimberger, author of *The New Single Woman*, and the American Association of Retired People's 2006 study of women ages 45 and older. They tell us that modern single women are for the most part happy, with satisfying lives; and they're content with the prospect of remaining single. They have fulfilling relationships either cohabiting with a partner or nonexclusive dating and they have strong friendship networks and deep connection with family and community. The majority of the AARP surveyed women (81%) are enjoying the freedom from caretaking others and see their later years as the chance to focus on themselves and do the things they've always wanted to do. Of course, for many of us, finding the right partner in later life means being with someone who supports us in what we're already doing—whether that means focusing on the things we've always wanted for ourselves or pursuing new dreams.

WHY ARE YOU SINGLE?

The question of *why* you are single might seem obvious to you, or it might be something you've been avoiding being truly honest about. Regardless of what's true for you, it's important to ask yourself this question and to get clear about the answer so that you can be proactive about what you want as you move forward.

My research has revealed that as much as we women think, dream, fantasize, and talk about romantic relationships, we don't realize where we're lacking clarity or what specifics we should consider in pursuit of a partner. We talk mostly about what we don't want rather than what we do want. Those negative thought patterns restrain us and keep us in a loop with the same pattern of disappointing relationships. So many of the women I interviewed didn't realize how necessary it was to create a clear vision of their ideal man. Instead, I often heard beliefs such as:

- *I'll never find that one man exactly right for me.*
- *All the good ones are taken.*
- *Men are too much work; I'm probably better off single.*
- *The men I meet are emotionally unavailable.*
- *All men are alike, I can't trust them.*
- *I'm not pretty enough (thin enough, young enough, smart enough) to meet the right man.*
- *I have to compete with younger women for the limited available men.*
- *If I have to be the one who changes instead of the man, I quit.*
- *A good relationship is hard work. If it takes this much work to have bad relationships, what will it take to have a good one!*
- *Nobody's perfect so I have to take the good with the bad, even if I don't get what I really want and need.*
- *I'm strong and don't really need much from a man.*

These are common beliefs, and perhaps one or more resonate with you. These beliefs reveal an explicit need for a new approach, and an emotionally creative process to envision and attract an ideal mate. Most women have never gone beyond writing a list of qualities they want in a man, if that. Many are confused about being too picky, how much to compromise, and what is unrealistic about their desires. They often complain about the peculiar and emotionally unavailable men they continue to meet through online dating services, blind dates, and elsewhere. For many women, real life experience reinforces these belief systems until we assume there just aren't any good men out there anymore. We get frustrated and burned out on the dating game. And legitimately so! If this speaks to you, then you're about to step into the reality of creating your own Dream Man story and attracting him into your life. There may be many reasons why you haven't settled into a life partnership, including:

- You're consumed by a demanding (and perhaps fulfilling) career.
- You maintain high standards for the kind of man you want, but lack the tools to know how to find him.
- You've been enjoying being footloose and not tied to anyone else.
- You're ambivalent about the whole notion of marriage and settling down.
- You have only witnessed poor relationship models, and you're skeptical that anyone can experience a successful, loving, long-term partnership.
- You're already feeling like a failure when it comes to love, and you're afraid to allow yourself the possibility you may be hurt again.

JAN'S STORY:
One Day I Woke Up Single—Now What?

Let me tell you about Jan. She is forty-nine and has never been married or had children or even dated much. She loves her career and that's where her attention had been, until her last birthday. She realized life was passing quickly and she began soul-searching and questioning why she had chosen the single life and whether it was a mistake. Since our culture is so family-oriented, she said she felt somewhat relegated to an unimportant role in life. Many parents she met over the years told her that raising their kids had been the most important thing they'd ever done, and it seemed to Jan that it gave them a feeling of significance. Feeling it was too late for her to have children, she realized that she wanted to feel a sense of her own purpose by sharing her life with a partner, and yet, she pondered, "How does someone my age, who isn't exactly a beauty queen, meet anyone?"

Jan feels like many women who come to this conclusion, women who don't have a clue about navigating the dating world, including the ominous prospect of online dating. They have crushing thoughts like, "It's too late," or "I'm too old," or "I don't know if I could share my life after being single for so long." I want to reach out to any and all of you who might feel this way and let you know that there is hope, and a way to create the life you want, even at a mature age. I've met women who found their dream partner in their seventies and eighties. There's a Dream Man for every woman.

So now back to the question of why you're single. It may be something you take for granted, something you don't even ponder. Regardless, I encourage you to do a quick self-examination and see if there are any surprising answers floating around in your subconscious. Just jot down anything that comes to mind when you ask yourself: *Why am I single?*

I'm single because... _____

_____

_____

_____

_____

_____

_____

_____

_____

_____

_____

_____

_____

_____

_____.

You might find your answer is a mixed bag of conscious choices and old limiting beliefs. As I mentioned earlier, your intuition knows something is wrong with the mating game, but you're uncertain what to do about it. We can create different results if we change limiting beliefs and perceptions of what is possible. I'm going to show you how to dream the possible dream.

PART 2. How to Get the Most Out of This Book

"With your dream man, you become more of who you are and who you aspire to become."

GIVE YOURSELF TIME—YOU DESERVE IT

Dedicating the time and space required to move through the Choose Him Process is key to getting the unparalleled value this book has to offer. It's truly worth an investment of introspective you-time. After all, this is about your life and what you really want. It's important for you to know up front that this process will involve some contemplative thinking. It might take you several sittings of concentrated time to complete the process, especially since it's about you and your love life. What you're going to get is hugely important. It's not only clarity about yourself—it's clarity about what you want deep inside, and living your dream life with the man of your dreams.

A NEW WAY TO CHOOSE YOUR PARTNER

At this point you may be rearing to go—and I don't blame you! If you want to move onto Step 1 of the Choose Him Process, you're absolutely free to do so. But I also encourage you to read the section that follows, whether you do it now or later, as it offers valuable background information about how we got here in the first place. I'm proposing that there's a new way through to the future of healthy, harmonious partnerships. It's based on identifying and clearing out our old ways of thinking and replacing them with something new. It's about being authentic and empowered in relationship and drawing to you men who think this is sexy and irresistible rather than threatening. Do you think this sounds like a pipedream? I assure you—it's not. I've witnessed women go through this process and let go of their negative thinking only to attract the very relationship they hadn't dared to want.

It's important for you to know that this process can bring up some pain and discomfort. It may even reveal some belief systems we wish we didn't have—or didn't know we had. But mostly it's meant to be fun. As much as it's about finding your Dream Man, it's also all about you. It's a process for getting to know yourself better, and for understanding where you're coming from so that you can become a powerful creative force in your own life. What could be better than that?

Much will be revealed as you go, particularly for those of you who are mired in pessimistic beliefs about men and the possibility that you can have what you really want. If this is true for you, I strongly encourage you to read the next section before jumping ahead. It's genuinely important for us all to understand the cultural conditions that set the stage for where so many of us find ourselves today.

For those of you who are ready to go, take a deep breath and start to feel the possibilities of creating the vision, the man, the partnership, and the life you've always dreamed of.

PART 3. *How Did We Get Here?*

> "Our future is in our ability to create authenticity-based, harmonious relationships. It's up to us."

RELATIONSHIP PARADIGMS

Paradigms are mental models and frameworks through which we see our world or reality. They are cultural belief systems that act as automatic filters for our perceptions, causing us to think and behave in certain ways. Paradigm shifts occur when society, as a collective whole, begins to behave from a new set of beliefs. For example, in the 1960s, during the anti-establishment movement, young people began to view sex and "free love" as their right, and the shifts that happened as a result of that time have had long-lasting cultural, social, and behavioral ramifications that inform the way we think and act today. Similarly, at that time there was radical dissent against the Vietnam War, and African Americans and women began to take powerful stands for their rights. These groups questioned and even revolted against religious dogma, and educational, social, and political doctrine. In other words, they made strong statements about the need to re-evaluate the foundation of our beliefs, practices, values, and behaviors in all aspects of our lives. And it worked. They caused major social change that is impacting us to this day.

Paradigm shifts typically occur through these types of upheavals and rebellions; as a result of scientific discoveries, technological advances; and because of social and business revolutions that we see leading to global expansion and interdependence. These shifts are how we evolve as a human race, hopefully for the better. In recent decades, things seem to be changing so rapidly that it's hard to see where we're still operating from outdated paradigms. We forget to question the validity and current relevance of some of our beliefs and practices, oftentimes because it's simply easier to continue with the same thoughts and the same way we've always done things. Especially if there is no specific cataclysmic event or uprising, there is nothing to wake us  up and force us to update our belief systems and personal patterns of thought and behavior. There haven't been any riots or government intervention mandating that we upgrade our relationship software. This explains why our romantic relationship paradigms have not shifted and evolved to match our social evolution. Stick with me on the following topics because they're related to the "man channel" and what's keeping you from having what you want.

THE POWER OF CHOICE

Do you value choice? I'm talking about your options, alternatives, personal preferences, sumptuous selections, diverse elections, and unlimited possibilities. Consider how different it feels to shop in an abundant farmers' market with plentiful choices versus having to make do with scraps you had to pull from a dumpster to feed your family. If a trashcan was your only choice, you would experience a sense of scarcity and not enough, compromise, sacrifice for others, humiliation, low self-esteem, self-criticism, low energy, fear, and hopelessness. On the other hand, the abundant market would give you a sense of unlimited supply, confidence that you will find what you want, and the natural awareness that you can decide what you want, select the best, and be satisfied with your choices. Women have this power of choice in every decision we make, but many of us feel (consciously or unconsciously) more like we're standing at the edge of that dumpster when it comes to our romantic options.

Taking a look back through our history will uncover unexamined beliefs. These old and ingrained paradigms constitute our sense of limited choices. For thousands of years, women have

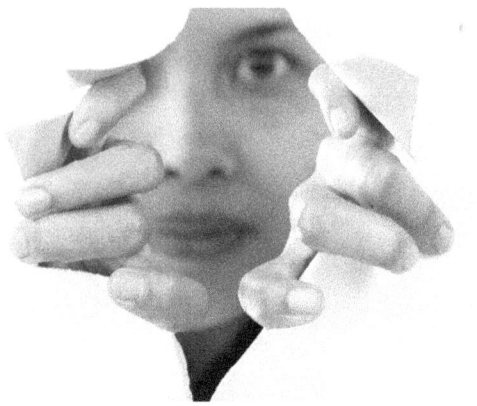 suffered discrimination, humiliation, and abuse due to the perception that we are the physically and intellectually inferior gender who must depend on men for our survival. Until the mid-twentieth century, most women's primary goal in life was to be married, raise a family, and be provided for by a man. They had to relegate their own wishes and cater to the needs of their men. Alongside the pervasive paradigm of inequality, women's natural nurturing and caregiving instincts, coupled with their desire for security, shaped their behavioral patterns of compromise, sacrifice, self-denial, and low self-worth, all of which led to seeking approval from men. Most of these women had no choice. By today's standards, they were controlled, judged, devalued, and disrespected within the accepted paradigms of those times. It is no wonder that many women have to work through a strong inclination for "people-pleasing."

Now, I'm going to take a big leap here, but I'm going to suggest that too many of us are subconsciously carrying the residual survival patterns of our mothers and female ancestors. It was only a few generations ago that we got the right to vote, and only thirty years ago that the Equal Rights Amendment for nondiscrimination on the basis of sex was introduced. My own mother experienced tremendous adversity growing up in the South in the 1930s and '40s. Marriage was her only legitimate means of survival. I personally carried many of her deep-rooted beliefs and patterns, many of which spurred my quest for my own identity, authentic power, and wholeness. Women's rapid advancement in many arenas this past century, through legal regulation and political activism, has enabled us to achieve new levels of financial independence and self-determination. But through my years of research, discussions, observations, and coaching women, it is apparent that the energy of inequality and limited choices still resides in us. There is no one group to be blamed. Certainly men cannot be responsible for solving an impediment so deeply embedded in women's psyche when most women are not conscious of these subtle, programmed limitations.

BREAKING THROUGH LIMITATIONS

So how do we change programmed limitations? The first step is awareness, just recognizing they exist and that they control our feelings and our decisions. The next step is knowing what is true about you, what you feel, and what you truly want; then you make decisions from this place of clarity. We experience feelings, emotional reactions, and process our thoughts based on our beliefs, and we make choices and decisions from those points of view. For example, you might find yourself very attracted to a blue-collar man, and you are in a professional management position. You may automatically eliminate him as a potential partner because of your belief that you must have a man of the same educational, financial, and social status as yours. You assume that he must not be educated and he must not have a high enough social or financial status due to his career choice. When you get new information, however, you can change your beliefs, which in turn changes your feelings about things. For instance, after an extended conversation, you might find out that this man is very intelligent, confident, and secure in who he is, and that he's traveled a great deal and decided to do the work he loves instead of pursuing a professional career. He may suddenly seem more interesting and attractive and your feelings about him change. You then realize that you made a snap judgment based on superficial observations, so you decide he could be a potential partner. You learned from this experience to not be so quick to judge a book by its cover. When you change your beliefs, and therefore your feelings, you see your choices differently, and you make more informed, new decisions.

This book provides you with some new information and perspectives that can help you see your options in new ways and help you make more informed decisions about yourself and for yourself. Throughout this book, you will find many references to outdated ways of thinking, many in the form of women's personal stories and revelations. You may even be surprised to uncover your own limited belief systems and find that they are keeping you trapped in paradigm prisons. We are not held there against our will. The prison doors are unlocked and all we have to do is walk through them.

The work you'll be doing in this book is about more than exposing our outdated beliefs and relationship paradigms. It's also a logical and sensible approach to intentional transformation and conscious choices. By introducing an evolved concept for partner selection, this book provides guidance on how to allow your energetic compatibility to take the lead in how you attract men to you. Your energetic compatibility has to do with that magnetic resonance, or energetic echo, I mentioned in the introduction to this book. In other words, what are you resonating into the world about what you want. Energetic compatibility includes core desires and needs, complementary values, lifestyles, ways of handling conflict, intimacy, and communication. When you have energetic compatibility across these qualities, you will have a relationship in which you're being supported to be your true and authentic self—and you're doing likewise for your man. It's past time that we base our long-term relationships on realistic guidelines and expectations consistent with our evolution and circumstances today. Our society is in love with romance because it feels really good—temporarily. We worship the uncontrollable feeling of connecting and melding our energies into magical union with faith that love will conquer all. The exquisite harmony we experience with sexual chemistry is often mistakenly believed to lead to harmony in all aspects of the relationship. It's clear we need to reorient ourselves from hormonally induced romantic fantasy to authenticity-based romantic reality. And we do have the choice.

THE POWER OF AUTHENTICITY

When I talk about coming from an authenticity-based romantic reality, I'm talking about being genuine and having integrity in your relationships by acting in a way that is true to yourself and your beliefs. Authenticity is when your thoughts, words, feelings, and actions are in alignment. You don't confuse yourself and others with mixed messages and energy. Any time something feels natural and not forced, or doesn't create a sense of discomfort or negative emotions, it's a sign that you are being authentic and true to yourself. When you're consistent in your expression, you know what you stand for and you're more centered, calm, and clear. To be true to yourself in this way means speaking your mind and letting others know how you feel and what you want. It's not possible to attract or be in an authenticity-based romantic relationship when you aren't clear about what you want.

My definition of authentic personal power is when conscious choices and decisions are made from a place of present-moment awareness and clarity:

knowing what you feel, what you want, what is real, and what is really happening—and then taking responsibility for your own experiences and the outcomes. When you're authentic, you do things because you want to fully express yourself in every way and live from an honest place within yourself. That is being true to yourself and honest with others about who you really are. When you do this, you give space to live from a place of greater capacity and self-awareness that you may have wanted but have not explored until now. You will finally let go of the attitude that you have to settle or compromise your desires. When you do this, you begin to more fully live your potential, and you can start to better appreciate what you have to offer. Others will also see and respond to you more positively, since it's obvious you're acting in integrity and alignment with the real you. You'll begin to attract more of what you want in all your relationships and your life. I invite you to ask yourself how authentic and vulnerable you're allowing yourself to be in your relationships.

AUTHENTICITY IS THE NEW GAME—GET REAL

The Choose Him Process will guide you to find your way back to authenticity and genuine personal power. Our media and culture focus on superficial images of beauty and stereotypical behaviors for women and men. And it's not easy to escape assaults to our self-esteem by the continual onslaught of messages aimed at making us feel insecure so we'll keep buying more products, reading more magazines, and watching more TV. We can't walk into a store without seeing negative magazine headlines about women's bodies, relationship make-ups and break-ups, and ways to tantalize men to want us. Many of us have been caught up in looking to the media to tell us how to look, how to think, how to be. It strengthens the message that negative drama in people's lives is normal, and it's not. We're ready for a change. Much of the current material related to dating and finding an ideal mate is based on antiquated models. They instruct us how to play the *game*, follow the *rules*, and manipulate men through snappy repartee, feigned self-control, false self-confidence, and strategies for *winning* his heart and *hooking* him into marriage. While many of these resources suggest useful tips and more empowered ways to interact with men, they are still derived from and perpetuate an outdated perspective. Most also reinforce the artificial notion of scarcity of available men. I'm embarrassed by the archetypal characterizations of women as desperate, irrational, and pining for men who don't want them. Too many of the women I've interviewed feel they have to be the one to change their life to adapt to a man's life, which is why they're often frustrated and many just give up the search for a mate. Their intuition tells them there is something wrong with this picture, but they don't know what to do about it. This process is a way through this frustration.

OLD PARADIGMS TO NEW

Changing paradigms requires a compelling shift in human consciousness. The so-called battle of the sexes is so last millennium! This outdated gender battle the media likes to hook us into inherently demands power, force, and control over one another. This wasted energy must end. It traps us in senseless, unending conflict and drama that inhibits personal evolution. We need to update and reshape our paradigms to balance masculine and feminine energies. We need to advocate for roles in which men and women live harmoniously in pursuit of higher human ideals.

Our current dysfunctional relationship models and mating patterns do not match our social evolution, but that's for a future book. However, take a look at the following example of our current outdated mating paradigms as opposed to where we ought to be headed in order to be living from an evolved model. The full comparison is in the Appendix.

OUTDATED FANTASY/CHEMISTRY ATTRACTION	EVOLVED REALITY/ENERGETIC COMPATIBILITY ATTRACTION
• Mate selection is based on temporary, hormonally-induced and lust-driven attraction • Stereotypical attraction factors based on image, surface attributes and perceptions • Cultural and media-driven stereotypes of beauty and desirability • Initial passion and lust fuel unsustainable fantasy roles (i.e. knight in shining armor rescues princess and they live happily "ever after") • Physical appearance (image) and external/surface qualities take precedence over long-term compatibility • False assumption that long-term compatibility will automatically follow chemical compatibility (Divorce statistics prove otherwise) • Female is chosen by male • Male decides and "surprises" female with proposal (often under pressure from her)	• Mate selection is primarily based on harmonious feelings and essence compatibility between partners • Lust and chemistry attraction is secondary to long-term compatibility factors • Beauty & desirability defined individually & stereotypes are viewed as caricatures • Reality-based roles and long-term compatibility considerations take priority • Long-term compatibility & energetic resonance takes precedence over external/surface qualities • Energetic compatibility (includes essence, core desires, shared values, lifestyles, and ways of handling conflict, intimacy, and communication) • Coupling / marriage is a mutual decision • Proposal ritual is a formality and celebration
Results in: **Limited available partner choices through hasty judgmental exclusion of candidates; dominant / submissive pattern.**	Results in: **Expanded available partner choices through broader selection criteria based on energetic compatibility; partnership pattern.**

This is the age of personal potential for both women and men who desire more harmony, joy, meaning and purpose in their lives. Women can lead the way by shedding old beliefs and patterns in ourselves and our relationships and realizing that we have options for intentional partnering. Are you ready to choose the shift?

THE MAN TRAP GAME

A woman's pursuit of romantic partnering should never be a contest to *win* a man. We are not hunters lying in wait to *trap*, or fisher(wo)men trying to *hook* men. After we *catch* him, what then? We begin commiserating with our girlfriends and buying books on how to deal with troubled relationships. At the root of this dilemma is our buying into outdated and false perceptions of ourselves and expectations in romantic partnering—the so-called battle of the sexes. Why does it have to be a fight? Why aren't harmonious relationships the norm? Let's begin by shifting our collective consciousness—our group mentality—to transform the foundation of the problem instead of continuing to accept and function under this old paradigm. Since women no longer have to partner for survival, we no longer need to employ antiquated strategies and feminine wiles to *capture* or hold onto a man. Let's wake up, get real, self-loving, and true to our natural inner wisdom.

SELENA'S STORY:
How She Fell into False Survival Mode

Selena is an accomplished and successful businesswoman in her mid forties who'd raised a son and was married for the second time to a very controlling man named Joe. They had no children together and kept their finances separate, so there were none of the usual trappings that hold couples together when the relationship is no longer working. As with most controlling men, Joe progressively alienated Selena from her friends, family, employees, and even her son. He convinced her that they were all selfish users, gossips, incompetent, and even dangerous. Their relationship became just Joe and Selena.

She felt powerless to defend her opinions and ask for what she needed. He turned it into something that was her problem, not his. Even as a successful entrepreneur, she began to feel helpless, losing her self-esteem and confidence in her ability to make decisions. She was not actually living in survival mode, but that's how she felt and how she was behaving. She thought she had no choice because of her ingrained belief that no other man would want her at her age. So she needed to hold on tight to this man to feel good about herself. Ironically, the opposite happened. Selena became depressed and soon her once lively eyes had dark shadows that seemed to say to the world that the woman who once lived here is dead. There was no light in her, as if her energy and spirit had left her body. She needed to refill herself and revitalize her energy by facing what was happening to her and getting clear about what she wanted, and then making a decision to leave. When she finally did, her spirit, personality, competence, and lightness returned to her body. She regained her personal power and realized she alone was in charge of her choices and decisions. Selena then defined what she wanted in a future partnership that would be mutually respectful, caring, and supportive, and she went on to meet and marry her Dream Man two years later!

CHOOSING THE SHIFT

Let's start with ourselves. In this book we'll be examining our personal perspectives, principles, and self-perceptions as part of the process of getting clear. Only when we get real and honest with ourselves can we change our expectations and make choices and decisions based on what we know to be true in our hearts. We must lift our own veils of illusion and see what is real and what is really happening rather than just accept conventional wisdom or what has always been. I'm going to be encouraging you to take a serious look at your old belief systems and to move forward with new beliefs that will help you get in touch with your highest values and to trust your powerful feminine intuition. It's up to you to create what you want and redefine your foundational beliefs. Once you've started that process, you'll be amazed at how freeing it is to let go of the old belief systems and move forward from a place of active choice rather than passive acceptance.

LADIES' CHOICE AND THE NEW PRINCE CHARMING

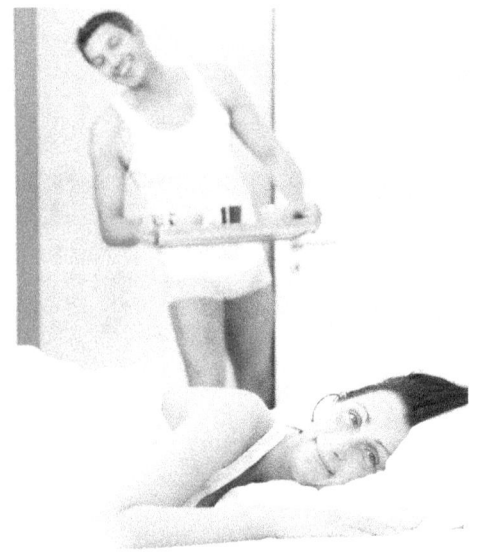

Many women believe that relationships are built on fate and happenstance, as in fairytales and romantic novels. As girls, many of us grew up watching movies that reinforced the Cinderella story, depicting women waiting for Prince Charming to sweep her off her feet and choose her, among all the women fighting for his attention and approval, to be his wife. As we mature, the fantasy begins to fade and we think we must compromise and settle for less and that we'll be lucky if a man comes along with even a few of the qualities we really want. Some of us even go into competition with other women in the hope that the glass slipper will fit us alone.

Why do we think we have to be chosen by a man? I've mentioned that this is an antiquated way of thinking. It's true that history, and some cultures in today's world, operate under this paradigm where the man chooses. But today, in our society, women have permission to be ourselves. Men are craving equal partners, and the idea that we have to be compromising, seductive, manipulative, and competitive with other women in order to gain a man's attention is as damaging for men as it is for us!

The new model today is that we get to decide what works for us and we have choices. In other words, "I have my own damn slippers, and I want to know if we're compatible dance partners!" Partnering is a mutual decision for mutual joy and fulfillment.

Yet today women still often wait (plead, demand, fight) for the man to propose as if it is his sole decision to marry us. Did you know that you get to choose him, too? That statement seems obvious, but there remains a subtle, underlying belief in most women that we have to be chosen by a man; hence, we unconsciously relinquish our power of choice to him. Regardless of their successful professional or financial status, many women have confided to me that they look for validation from men. Perhaps what women are really looking for are men who value them as equals and their mutual potential to pursue their aspirations. The fact is that we can and must determine our own ideals and requirements and decide if he is truly what we want. Here's a new perspective: What if your modern prince is less of a charmer and more authentic, a true partner who recognizes and supports you in expressing your own authenticity and potential? What if it's up to us women to teach men how to regard us, love us, and support us in our dreams? We can show them how by becoming authentic, clear, and honest about what we want, accompanied by the resonating inner knowing that we deserve it.

UNVEILING YOUR FULL POTENTIAL

What does our potential have to do with finding a Dream Man? Our potential represents all of our underlying possibilities, capabilities, brilliance, talents, and hidden desires for self-expression, meaning, and purpose in life. Women today are smart, talented, capable, and get great satisfaction from accomplishments and pursuing goals and dreams. Many women experience concern about whether a man will understand and place value on her needs and aspirations. Again, referring back to programmed limitations and paradigms, there is an undertone of confusion and often conflict around how many of her own dreams will have to be relegated below her man's. In an evolved partnership, women and men value freedom for individual choices and self-expression and support each other in achieving their highest potential.

Your potential can be as simple as carrying the essence of feminine values, such as the energy of optimism, love, joy, wisdom, and compassion for others in your way of being and doing your life. Or it could show up in a creative endeavor or something that has positive impact on others' lives, your community, society, or the world. Expressing our potential fills the neglected void in our hearts that says there is something more for us to know, to be, to experience, to create, or to do while we're here. Each one of us is significant, valuable, and essential on this earth. Women have remarkable intellectual, creative, and humanistic gifts that can make the world a better place. We're practical, holistic thinkers with get-it-done attitudes. Let's start by realizing we can use that same energy to intentionally design our partnerships to support us in becoming all we are meant to be. Now, let's move on to exactly how this entire process works.

THE LAW OF ATTRACTION AND DEEPLY INGRAINED BELIEFS

The Law of Attraction says that you have the power to attract whatever you want into your life. The premise is that all your thoughts, all the visions and imagery in your mind, and all the feelings connected to your thoughts will later manifest as your reality. The Law of Attraction tells us that everything you've attracted into your life so far has been a direct result of your thoughts, conscious and subconscious beliefs, and *your feelings*.

Since you haven't had success in finding the right man, it's likely that some of your thoughts, beliefs, and emotions are not allowing him into your life. For example, if you have an unconscious belief that men are not to be trusted, or that having a man will restrict your independence, your chances of attracting and creating a lasting and fulfilling relationship are highly diminished. That negative belief creates a magnetic attraction in your energy field that brings you exactly what you're trying to avoid—men you can't trust or controlling men. You also are likely to see repetitive patterns in the men you attract and in your relationships.

INVITATION TO LIBERATION

You don't have to be frustrated—get clear, authentic, and intentional instead! Free yourself from outdated paradigms. There is a Dream Man for every woman! You attract into your life experience what your deepest beliefs and moment-to-moment thoughts create.

This means having a positive thought and as a result feeling inspired, exuberant, excited, stimulated, elated, enthusiastic, euphoric, appreciated, proud, safe, content, calm, warm, peaceful, free, happy, and so on. Those are the good feelings to use as your filter throughout writing the story of your Dream Man. Soak up the good feelings as you describe your dream relationship. That is how you get what you want. I believe that what you clearly define in writing, trust in your heart, and embody with feelings will come to you. Combining the Choose Him Process and the Law of Attraction is like installing a turbo charge—a double-dose magnetic energy that will super charge you in manifesting what you want.

When you get clear and authentic about who you are, and when you get intentional about what you want in your Dream Man, you will attract the man who is a mirror of your new embodied beliefs! This is authentic personal power in action. That is what this book is all about. The only way you can inhibit the connection with your Dream Man is to continue holding onto old beliefs, negative thoughts and patterns, and outdated paradigms.

There are three simple steps in this Choose Him Process: (1) Reflecting on who you are, what you value, and your belief systems and history so you can get clear about what you want moving forward; (2) Creating the man of your dreams by defining what you want in writing from your heart and feelings; and (3) Manifesting the outcome in your real life.

By going forward with this process, I invite you to commit to:

- uncovering and transforming your thought patterns, beliefs, and behaviors.
- creating the story of a Dream Man who complements your needs and values and who can appreciate who you are authentically.
- attracting a man who loves you unconditionally and fulfills your dreams.
- claiming your own personal power through the journey of creating your Dream Man and your dream life.

PART 4. The Choose Him Process

"Authenticity is the new sexy!"

IT'S A TRANSFORMATIONAL TOOL

The Choose Him Process is a self-discovery and self-coaching tool that can help you in many ways. You will:

- **get clear about who you are**, what you love, what you value, and what you truly want in a man and a relationship.

- **be inspired into action** and release blocks or mental paradigms that might be in the way of attracting your Dream Man.

- **reconnect with your feelings** and be reminded of who you are at your core, leaving self-worth and self-esteem problems behind.

- **set standards** for expectations of your man and for your life together, including your personal dreams and aspirations.

- **express your deepest desires** in relationship and learn to relinquish the need to prove your value to a man.

- **realize that you can choose the man of your dreams** and shift your perspective from waiting to be chosen.

- **be empowered with a new resource** to help you envision and attract the man of your dreams from a strong, deserving place where your identity is self-defined, separate, and complementary to a man's.

As you continue, your thoughts, beliefs, feelings, and way of being will evolve. This process integrates the Law of Attraction with your heart-centered story and what I call magnetic resonance, meaning you will be attracting a man who is energetically compatible with you.

THE STEPS

The process for creating your story and attracting your Dream Man is made up of three major steps:

1. Reflect—discovering, exploring, taking inventory of your past and present, and changing beliefs.

2. Create—using the creator tool to design the story for your Dream Man.

3. Attract—attracting the man of your dreams by bringing him to life.

Consider breaking this process up into several sittings according to your stamina. Reset the stage and atmosphere for doing the work each time you come back to it.

For all of the activities that follow, you don't have to fill in every blank, and you can attach more pages if you need to. This is your story and you are the creator. Once you've finished the entire process, you'll be guided through how to turn it into your final story. When you read the finished story from start to finish, you will feel a difference and know that you have shifted your way of thinking, feeling, and being!

A FEW CAUTIONS

Because this is a transformational process, as you do the following personal exploration activities and complete your Dream Man story, you may experience some of the following symptoms:

- anxiety
- dizziness or a whirly feeling in your head
- drowsiness or tiredness
- headache
- nausea
- sweaty palms
- anything else that you typically experience under stress

Please don't be alarmed or think this process isn't for you. If you do experience any of these symptoms, they're often caused by your mind's reaction to assimilating new information and to exploring and possibly shifting your beliefs. It may also be your internal resistance to change or possibly to the anticipation that you can actually have what you deeply want. Breathe through this and relax. Symptoms will fade as you integrate new information, change your perceptions, and finally start to believe that you can have the man of your dreams. He's out there waiting for you.

STEP 1. *Reflect—It's All About You*

> "Being true to yourself is the key to having the man of your dreams."

This section is filled with space for you to empty your man-baggage and declare who you are, what you love and value, and your primary motivation for wanting the man of your dreams. This preparation work will set the tone for creating your Dream Man story. Remember, the Choose Him Process is ALL about YOU. Allow one to three hours to complete this first section.

OUT WITH THE OLD AND IN WITH THE TRUE YOU

Whether you like to think about it or not, you carry old beliefs that are potentially lodged in your psyche from your past experiences, family, and society. They can hinder rather than promote growth and intimacy, as well as limit your options concerning men. It's incredibly freeing to get your beliefs out in the open!

BETWEEN YOU AND ME: *Taking the Backseat*

For most of my life I actually believed it was my role to disregard or subordinate my dreams to focus primarily on my man's goals—regardless of my growing personal and professional worth. It was an unconscious belief, but his success took precedence over mine, and I relegated my aspirations to a secondary position. My Dream Man has helped me to understand how immense that sacrifice truly was by being such a big supporter of my dreams.

Other old beliefs that may now be outdated include your inherited religious background. We all know this has an impact on our choice of a mate. We acquire our beliefs from our culture, families, religion, media, and past experiences, among many other factors. No matter where you stand in your faith or spiritual beliefs, some of the concepts we hold to be true in this arena may be overdue for some introspection. This is a great opportunity to clear out any feelings and ideas about things you've been questioning or which no longer serve you and to replace them with new thoughts so you can move into a new phase of attracting the man who is right for you. For example, perhaps you want to attract a man of your religious faith because your parents had always expected you to do so. If you weren't holding on to that parental expectation, would you still want to make the same choice?

What are some of your parents' beliefs or judgments about religion, race, political perspective, social status, etc.? How have they affected your dating choices? Do you want to continue to give them the power to influence your life choices? Do these influences create feelings of harmony or stress in your body?

_____
_____
_____
_____
_____
_____
_____
_____
_____
_____.

BETWEEN YOU AND ME: *X-Ray Vision*

I had an old belief and judgment that most men who dressed and behaved conservatively were too nice, or were boring conformists with narrow viewpoints. Was I wrong! I now describe my husband as the man who at first appeared to be a conservative Clark Kent and surprised me when he transformed into Superman. He is more broadminded and has had a far more adventurous and interesting life than I would have ever imagined at first glance. So don't be fooled by the external package. By focusing on the priorities in my Dream Man story, I expanded my limited preferences and opened my mind and heart to more possibilities. Before that, I wore psychological blinders and literally could not see him. My husband's office was in the building next to mine and we went to the same gym. He had noticed me ten years before we met, but I never noticed him. That is, not until after I did my Dream Man story.

Now let's explore some of your own old beliefs and discover which are the ones you most cling to about men. In the chart that follows, write one old belief on the left and its accompanying new belief on the right. Since facing the old beliefs can stir up some upsetting feelings, I recommend writing your old beliefs first and then writing out all the new beliefs with a fresh, positive intention. An important tool in attracting what you desire is using the language of attraction. All this means is that you state in positive language what you want, as if it already exists. Write your statement in the present tense and affirm its truth within your statement: (I have . . . , I found . . . , I am . . . , My man is . . . , etc.). Transform all your negative statements into positives. For example, change "I don't want men with anger issues" into "My man is easy-going and handles upsets rationally."

OLD BELIEF	NEW BELIEF
There are no good men left for me.	I found my Dream Man and he is perfect for me.
I have to acquiesce to a man, make him king of the home, and give up my freedom.	I have my freedom and a man who treats me like a queen.
There aren't men out there who will get it. *(They are too needy, don't want a woman who's independent, too critical, womanizers, only want young bodies, etc.)*	My man gets it; he is a true modern man who treats me with equality and love, and is faithful.

OLD BELIEF	NEW BELIEF

FEMININE INSTINCTS

In our culture, we've become disconnected from our feelings and more focused on the unending chatter in our minds. We assume our minds will guide us to clarity with logic. We have it reversed. Our feelings are our internal guidance system—they clue us in that something is really in sync or out of whack. Since our minds are just a data processing tool, our feelings should be guiding our minds in our decision-making processes. Our culture has long been dominated by masculine values, such as logic, factual knowledge, competition, and aggression, while demoting feminine values, such as empathy, compassion, collaboration, intuition, and joy. As a result, we're out of balance. Our feelings connect us to our hearts and inform our experience of life. They are the key to unlocking our authenticity and bringing us what we desire. It's time to re-balance our values by reclaiming our feminine feelings and intuition and tuning up our natural guidance system.

FEELINGS MAKE US REAL

Believe me, I know this is an emotional process. It's designed that way for a reason: Only through accessing your authentic, deepest feelings and desires can you create an accurate picture of what kind of lifemate you really want. So what about you—are you already sensing your emotions bubbling up, perhaps ready to spill out? A lot of us hold a belief that we don't deserve this kind of relationship, or that it's not possible. And yet, if some part of you didn't believe that it was possible, you wouldn't be engaging in this process. Have you harbored secret wishes about the kind of relationship you could have? What woman hasn't? If so, note some of your thoughts here.

_____

_____

_____

_____

_____
_____
_____
_____
_____.

SOME PAIN, BIG GAINS

While you're doing these activities, some patterns will come to the surface. Don't be hard on yourself if you have big revelations that you weren't aware of before. Some of you may already be aware of romantic tendencies and patterns that don't work for you, while others may discover a completely new awareness through this awakening process. At every challenging shift in my life that has eventually led to getting what I want, I've initially had an emotional or painful reaction. For example, I've left relationships that weren't working even though I still loved the guy. These were debilitating experiences that stretched my emotions between two places—the one I was in and the one where I knew I needed to go. Awareness is the first stage of clearing old beliefs and patterns and attracting more of what you want, but oftentimes it's not pretty. Once you shift your perception, you evolve your beliefs, and then new opportunities appear. Think of the liberating times in your life when you shifted from a limiting belief to a whole new way of seeing things, and note some of them here.

_____
_____
_____
_____
_____
_____
_____.

WHAT I DON'T WANT

It's often easier for us to identify what we *don't want* rather than what we do want because we've had a memorable and painful experience of what didn't work out for us. The goal of the Choose Him Process, however, is to gain clarity about what you *do want*. To get there, though, you're going to go back in time to examine themes and patterns in your relationships with men that didn't work for you. When you start to recognize the patterns in your relationships, you can see where you've compromised or devalued yourself in some way. This awareness opens the door to changing the pattern. Some classic patterns include: being his doormat, being abused in any way, looking for father figures, being distracted by his good looks, wanting to heal his emotional wounds, and submitting to someone who's jealous and controlling.

Here are some other examples from my clients:

MY AGE	HIS NAME	THEMES THAT DIDN'T WORK FOR ME
35–39	Eric	Didn't love himself, didn't really love me, didn't deal with money well, emotionally unavailable
41–44	Paul	Boring, low libido, homebody, advice-giver
45–46	Don	Needy, wanted to stay home and watch TV every night, didn't love his work or his life

Now it's your turn:

MY AGE	HIS NAME	THEMES THAT DIDN'T WORK FOR ME

Now let's delve even deeper. As you think about past relationships, contemplate these questions:

- Why did they fail?
- How did you feel about each person at the end of the relationship?
- What part did you play in the failure?
- How did your choices contribute to the demise?
- What aspects of the relationship were you blind to, what red flags did you ignore?
- Did you prolong a relationship after you sensed it was doomed?
- Have you ever thought that a mediocre or even a poor partnership was better than none at all?

WHAT I DO WANT

Next, we're going to explore the list of things you don't want and see them side-by-side with those things you do want. It's not necessary to fill in all the blanks, but do add more pages if needed. Then draw big X's through your DON'T WANT list so that you and the Universe are clear about what you DO WANT. Make sure to turn those negative thoughts about what you don't want into positive statements. This is how you'll begin to change your thoughts to prepare to create your Dream Man story, which of course is all about what you DO want.

Examples:

WHAT I DON'T WANT	WHAT I DO WANT (the opposite)
An emotionally unstable man	A man who's aware and conscious of his feelings
A self-centered, selfish man	An authentic, open, generous, and self-aware man
A man without a passion	A man passionate about life and doing fun things

Your Turn:

WHAT I DON'T WANT	WHAT I DO WANT (the opposite)

Did you remember to draw a line through all items on your DON'T WANT list? According to the Law of Attraction, it's essential to focus on what you *are* calling into your life versus what you're releasing from your life. So reread the good, juicy DO WANT column, and then move on to the next section.

BETWEEN YOU AND ME: *Be Careful What You Think About*

The more I focused on how I didn't want controlling men, the more I became a magnet for them. Once I defined what I wanted and started to focus on having an adaptable, easy-going man, the more those types of men showed up.

COME APART TO COME TOGETHER

You may have heard the phrase "chaos before order." It means that things often need to come apart so they can be put together in a new way that works better—and this includes your life. A practical example is cleaning your closet, which can be an overwhelming task. When you finally start the project and take everything out, it looks like an even bigger mess, yet you know that diving in and putting it back together is going to produce a satisfying and much-needed result. This process you're undergoing is like the Big Closet Cleanout. You're transforming stagnant energy and making decisions about what works for you and what doesn't work any longer. You may struggle with what to hold onto and what to send to Goodwill or the dumpster. Any major change is a decision that can initially be uncomfortable and your resistance may be strong. But when you finally make the shift, it feels great to reorganize your life in a fresh, new way. You feel a sense of orderliness, clarity, and lightness in your body.

THE TRUTH WILL SET YOU FREE

In the February 2008 issue of *O!* magazine, Martha Beck wrote a fascinating article, "Go Tell Alice," describing what happens when we try to create from a powerless place. In the following quote, she refers to creating from superficial ideals and lists versus creating from your core and essence:

"When you're operating from the Shallows, you see yourself as isolated and separate. Your behavior consists of running from things you dread and grasping onto things you desire... The magic lists people make in the Shallows reflect their obsession with stuff—getting it, keeping it ...Fortunately, below the crust of the Shallows is an aspect of consciousness I call the Core of Peace. We can reach this whether we're rich or poor, married or single, famous or totally unknown—in fact, we've already reached it, because it is our essence. Sadly, most of us never realize this. We're so obsessed with the Shallows that we lose touch with our Core. We experience the disconnection as an aching inner void, which we diligently try to fill with more Shallow goodies...When my clients are in the Shallows, I can tell that the dreams they describe just won't fly; when they're speaking from their Core, I feel a kind of 'click,' like a puzzle piece fitting in place, and I know I'll see their dreams come true."

This process is the exact opposite of being in the *Shallows*. When you create from your *Core* you're being true to yourself and clear about what you want deep down. When you embrace what's true (real to you) and give up what's not true (superficial), you free up energy to receive what you want most.

In order to clearly define and attract the man of your dreams, you must be in the right state of mind and heart, create from your core, *feel the feelings* of what your life will be like with this new Dream Man, and believe beyond a shadow of a doubt that he will arrive. Think of this process as an artichoke: you're peeling back layers (symbolic of limiting beliefs) to get to the heart and core of who you truly are. Then you'll be creating from a place that says you can have and you deserve whatever you allow yourself to receive.

IT'S ALL ABOUT WHO I AM AND WHAT I LOVE

It's critical that you know what you love and value and what your core essence is. When I speak of essence, I'm referring to your authenticity. What is true about you deep inside? When you strip away all the titles, roles, and activities you do, what remains is your inner core, heart, spirit, soul, ideals, and fundamental nature. Knowing yourself means being aware of your feelings, emotional reactions, and what you care about.

Once you've created new beliefs, you're ready to bring clarity to what you love and value. This allows you to create the story of what you want from a place of knowing who you are and what you want rather than who he might want you to be and what you should want. These activities are an important step in acknowledging who you are, what you value, and what's negotiable and nonnegotiable. Know thyself and attract the right man to you.

TIME TO TAKE A BREATHER

Whew! At this point, take a moment to reflect on your revelations and new thoughts. Now that you've taken a good look at where you've invested yourself in old, limiting beliefs and romantic patterns, next you'll get to examine your magnetic qualities and the beauty in you. This is the beginning of your exploration and acknowledgment of the TRUE YOU. If you've had additional insights beyond these topics, take time to note them here.

_____
_____
_____
_____
_____
_____

_____
_____
_____
_____
_____
_____
_____
_____
_____
_____
_____
_____
_____ .

WHO I AM

The purpose of this activity is to help you get centered in who you are in your essence as a human being and what you care about in life. It's far easier for other people to see the beauty in you when you can see it yourself. When I first did this exercise, I thought it was going to be difficult, but once I got started, it was fun and fulfilling. Recognize, receive, and embrace who you really are in your core. Make sure to describe only positive attributes.

One more important thing to consider: There are many facets of you, different sides that you show selectively to other people or maybe display only when you're alone. We sometimes think that we don't know who we are because we feel like several or many different people. Part of this is because society tells us that we're supposed to define ourselves by the things we do and accomplish. Being authentic, however, means allowing yourself to be dynamic and true to yourself. Give yourself permission to explore and express all of your aspects, styles, roles, talents, personalities, eccentricities, and aspirations. As we continue to uncover our authenticity, the definition of who we are continues to expand since we live in a cycle of self-discovery and exploration. It's a natural part of our current evolution and unique potential; and besides, we become more authentic, interesting, fulfilled, and have a lot more fun when we allow the full expression of ourselves to surface.

Contemplate the following questions and write down some thoughts about them in the space below:

- What do you wish people knew about you?
- What qualities do you suspect you may keep hidden from others?
- What aspects of your real self make you feel vulnerable?
- What traits do you wish others would value about you?
- What would your close friends be surprised to learn about you?

BEFORE YOU DIE

The statements below focus on internal qualities and states of being that form a person's character and approach to life. When you write your own I AM statements, omit external examples such as specific activities you do. This includes roles, such as mother, entrepreneur, caretaker, or volunteer. Internal qualities are descriptive of your essence and your spirit. Ironically, these are the things people often say about a person at their funeral. The purpose of this exercise is for you to focus on your internal qualities to express who you really are *before* you pass on. This is an opportunity to reacquaint yourself with you. When I first did this exercise, my head started to spin. At first it was difficult for me to separate the work I do and the things I've accomplished from who I am at my core and in my essence. Get started and really dig deep to pat yourself on the back. Acknowledge the true you. Here are a few examples of internal qualities:

- I am kind and generous.
- I am a hard worker.
- I am a good person.
- I am a good listener.
- I am funny.
- I am willing to change and grow.
- I am smart.
- I am spiritual.
- I am soft and feminine.

Anything goes as long as you mean it when you write it. As you complete the following statements, really feel the feelings of what it's like to access your true self, your authenticity. Fill in as many blanks below as you like or add more lines.

I am _____.
I am _____.
I am _____.
I am _____.
I am _____.
I am _____.
I am _____.
I am _____.
I am _____.
I am _____.
I am _____.
I am _____.
I am _____.
I am _____.
I am _____.
I am _____.
I am _____.
I am _____.
I am _____.
I am _____.
I am _____.
I am _____.
I am _____.
I am _____.
I am _____.

WHAT I LOVE

Now it's time to write out all the things you love about life, yourself, the world, things you love to do, places you love to visit. Unlike the previous activity, this one includes internal and external loves. Again, anything goes. Keep writing until you can't think of one more thing you love.

Examples:

- I love meeting new people.
- I love dancing.
- I love to make people laugh.
- I love knowing people of different cultures.
- I love mashed potatoes.
- I love tennis.
- I love my sisters.
- I love laughing.
- I love to walk.
- I love art and painting.
- I love to support people in achieving their dreams.

I love _____ .

I love _____ .

I love _____ .

I love _____ .

I love _____ .

I love _____ .

I love _____ .

I love _____ .

I love _____ .

I love _____ .

I love _____ .

I love _____ .

I love _____ .

I love _____ .

I love _____ .

I love _____ .

I love _____ .

I love _____ .

I love _____ .

I love _____ .

I love _____ .

I love _____ .

I love _____ .

I love _____ .

I love _____ .

I love _____ .

I love _____ .

I love _____ .

I love _____ .

I love _____ .

I love _____ .

I love _____ .

WHAT I VALUE

Now explore what you value in life. Again, the list could be endless. Here are some routes to access your own values. Contemplate:

- What do you long for, what's missing in your life?
- What do you never have enough time for?
- What do you always make a priority that gives you pleasure?
- What can you always summon physical energy for?
- What do you admire in others?
- What do you aspire to as a way of life?
- Given a month off, how would you spend it?
- What excites you, revs up your heart rate?

_____
_____
_____
_____
_____
_____
_____
_____
_____
_____
_____
_____
_____
_____
_____
_____.

Now you're ready to make your list of values. Keep writing until you've really connected with all the things you value in this world. Have fun.

Examples:

- I value freedom to do what I want when I want.
- I value alone time.
- I value adventures.
- I value family time.
- I value travel.
- I value financial security.
- I value a nice home.
- I value my work.
- I value time to paint.
- I value time to volunteer.
- I value intellectual conversations.
- I value walks in nature.

I value _____.

I value _____.

I value _____.

I value _____.

I value _____.

I value _____.

I value _____.

I value _____.

I value _____.

I value _____.

I value _____.

I value _____.

I value _____.

I value _____.

I value _____.

I value _____.

I value _____.

I value _____.

I value _____.

I value _____.

I value _____.

I value _____.

I value _____.

I value _____.

I value _____.

I value _____.

I value _____.

I value _____.

I value _____.

I value _____.

I value _____.

I value _____.

I value _____.

WHAT I VALUE IN A RELATIONSHIP

Now that you know who you are, the things you love, and the things you value, what do you value in a relationship? The previous exercises gave you abundant clues.

Examples:

- In a relationship, I value time together.
- In a relationship, I value time apart.
- In a relationship, I value shared responsibilities.
- In a relationship, I value meals together.
- In a relationship, I value fun adventures together.
- In a relationship, I value listening and talking.

In a relationship, I value _____
_____.

In a relationship, I value _____
_____.

In a relationship, I value _____
_____.

In a relationship, I value _____
_____.

In a relationship, I value _____
_____.

In a relationship, I value _____
_____.

In a relationship, I value _____
_____.

In a relationship, I value _____

_____.

In a relationship, I value _____

_____.

In a relationship, I value _____

_____.

In a relationship, I value _____

_____.

In a relationship, I value _____

_____.

In a relationship, I value _____

_____.

In a relationship, I value _____

_____.

In a relationship, I value _____

_____.

In a relationship, I value _____

_____.

In a relationship, I value _____

_____.

In a relationship, I value _____

_____.

Feel free to keep writing. Later on, once you attract him and feel traction in the relationship, this can be a great list to share with your Dream Man. Next we'll uncover why you want this relationship.

MY DEEPEST MOTIVATION FOR WANTING A RELATIONSHIP

This exercise prompts you to choose the one core reason you want to be in a relationship. Please be honest with yourself—no one is watching or judging you. You want to create a story that is from your heart and truth. Being honest with yourself about this question will help you create a vision of the man you truly want in your life. It will be far easier to establish and internalize your priorities knowing your deepest motivation. If not, you'll be sending mixed signals and repeating more of the same disappointing relationships. Oftentimes the frustration and bitterness we so often see in women and the confusion so often professed by men results from our inability to truly embrace the answer to this question. While several of these statements may apply to you, choose only ONE answer, the one that most resonates—or write your own.

Potential reasons for wanting a relationship might include:

- I want to be married, be a mother, and raise a family.
- I want a companion to share my life with.
- I want a partner to combine our finances for a better lifestyle.
- I want someone who values me for all that I am.
- I want a man who inspires and encourages me to pursue my purpose/my work.
- I want to love and be loved unconditionally.
- I want a partner to share in important life experiences.
- I want a man to make me feel alive and excited about life.
- I want a regular sexual partner.
- I want to feel safe and secure.
- I want intellectual stimulation and challenge.
- I want someone to grow old with.

...more>

- ♥ I want a man who's interested in having an equal partnership, in which we mutually support each other in our dreams.
- ♥ I want a man who supports me emotionally/financially/as a mentor.
- ♥ State your own, but refine it to just one reason.

My deepest motivation for wanting a relationship:

_____
_____
_____
_____.

This last exercise may have been very emotional for you, perhaps even overwhelming. Are you surprised by anything you uncovered? How does stating your truth make you feel?

_____
_____
_____
_____
_____
_____
_____.

INTENTIONAL VERSUS THROW OF THE DICE

Now that you've identified some of your old beliefs and opened yourself up to new ways of thinking, I want to encourage you to really dream big. Open your mind to the possibility that you can have exactly the sort of man who would fit into most, if not all, of your pictures of an ideal relationship. Stop and take a moment to really feel yourself move into a state of allowing, of opening to all possibilities. For those of you who need to feel in control, this may feel like a temporary surrender. That's okay. This process actually puts you in the driver's seat and gives you a stronger sense of controlling your life by being intentional rather than leaving it up to fate to determine chance encounters with men who appear in your life.

GET A NEW ATTITUDE

The Choose Him Process approaches romantic partnering by redefining your view of yourself, your role, your choices, and how you choose a partner. This awakening process is intended to shift your beliefs and orientation to a place of authentic personal power and to move away from contrived and superficial empowerment that is not sustainable. You might find that it moves you from the old perspective of trying to *catch* a man (through manipulation or determining what he wants and then temporarily becoming that) to the perspective of finding a compatible, energetic match for you that will lead to an authentic and lasting relationship.

FAYE'S STORY:
What Happened When I Realized I Really Do Get To Choose

"I woke up one day realizing that I was forty-eight years old and somehow the entire past decade had flown by and I'd forgotten to have a man in my life! My career and travel aspirations filled my mid-thirties and forties and I had the belief that one day my man would come. But I was still single. Oops, what happened? No one told me that if I didn't find a man in my thirties it would be a bit more challenging in my forties. So I resolved myself to being a single, independent woman and gave up searching for a man. I also held the belief that there was no way I would find anyone who would match my dream at my age, and who also lived close by. But then, I completed my Dream Man story and I began to know that I could actually have what I wanted!

The next thing I knew, men very close to my story began appearing. The first guy I dated was so close to my story I began to think, *This can't be happening! This might be the one!* He aggressively pursued me and he was pretty irresistible. Now, I could have gone down an old path and fallen head over heals in infatuation and bent over backwards to try to fit this guy's ideal; instead, I decided to stay in my own power, observe him, and make my own choices that really felt true to me. I have the power to choose and I have the choice not to choose! What a concept! I trusted my feelings and made all of my decisions by being true to myself, and I was not in a hurry but rather in pure observation. That felt really good to me. I knew I could have everything I wanted and that it would all be there when I was truly ready to choose. So I am continuing to date to see who else appears!"

STEP 2. Create — Your Dream Man Story Creator

> "You can and will attract your dream man by being your authentic self and knowing what you want."

WHY A STORY?

How successful have you been in attracting the man of your dreams? Is there a list of your Dream Man qualities lying dormant in a journal, hidden on your hard drive, or forgotten in your nightstand? Does this list beckon you to visualize your Dream Man, or is it collecting dust in the land of the Cinderella fantasy? Have you written it down and cast it to the wind with hopes that your Dream Man will just appear out of thin air and sweep you off your feet? I bet you'll agree that's not likely to happen. You now have a practical tool to help you get what you want.

A story transports us right to the heart of the matter and brings to life the qualities and contexts that we want to embrace and experience. Like a romantic novel, a story evokes emotion and stirs your heartstrings. This experience is not like an academic textbook that takes you into your logical, rational, and often misleading mind. Writing the story takes you out of your head (and the confusing mental analysis and mind chatter) and into your heart, where your true core desires are seated.

A romantic story brings you to the present moment and connects you to your heart, bringing the true feelings and reality to your vision. A story creates an emotional experience coupled with a clear vision that invokes the Law of Attraction. Your vision can become reality through the Law of Attraction and magnetic resonance.

TURN YOURSELF ON

Creating your Dream Man story is designed to evoke positive feelings about the qualities you want in a man and the life you want to experience with him. It clarifies what you truly want, while simultaneously connecting you to the feeling of the experience of your desires. That is the real **secret to attraction**. A clear vision infused with experiencing the feelings of actually having what you want creates a powerful electromagnetic force that attracts your deepest desires. Simply put: *This is what I want and this is what it feels like to have it.* These are the clear, energetic signals you want to send out so that you get back what you want. You can think of *magnetic resonance* as your positive energetic echo—the energy that you emanate which attracts complementary or matching energy.

How can you expect to find your Dream Man if you haven't fully explored what your dream truly is? What is your energy resonating, and what mixed signals are you sending out that are keeping you from your man? If you want to be empowered to create the life you want, it's your responsibility to get clear and real about what you want. If you don't, you'll continue to experience disappointing relationships and you will not find a dream match.

Time for a quick check-in. I encourage you to take an honest reading of the energy you've been projecting—both about and towards men. What responses have you received? If this is too tough, ask a trusted friend to be candid about how she sees the kind of energy you've been emanating lately.

_____
_____
_____
_____
_____
_____.

THE WARMUP

Whether you're feeling excited or intimidated by the process at this point, allow whatever's present for you to come to the surface. It's important to access the truth of your emotional energy before you begin the next part of this process, the Choose Him Process. Let me give you some glimpses of what I wrote about my Dream Man in my own story—all of which are true about my wonderful husband:

- He's taller than me in my three-inch pumps, has strong arms, and gives huge bear hugs.
- He has charisma and radiates warm energy.
- Everyone thinks he's a nice guy and he really is.
- He listens to me without making me feel foolish about my thoughts.
- He's a good sounding board without trying to solve every problem for me with quick answers.
- He loves me and accepts me as I am.
- We respect each other's independent nature.
- We inspire each other to be the best we can be.

Start to think about some of the qualities you want that may have just popped into your mind while reading through this list. Take a look below at a sample of a Dream Man story.

SAMPLE DREAM MAN STORY

This example is included so that you can have a sense of what your final story might look like. This is a word-for-word completion of a sample Dream Man story created by one of my clients. Please note the use of the language of attraction, which stems from the Law of Attraction. This means the sample story uses positive language and depicts things as if they already exist. Therefore, it is told in the present tense. This is an important part of the process because it allows you to touch into the emotion of feeling what it will feel like once you've created your own story. Of course, yours will be customized to your own responses, but this will give you a taste of what your story might look like once you compile all your responses.

My Dream Man is between thirty-eight and forty-five years old since I prefer a man closer to my age. He is about five-foot-nine to six-foot-one, which matters to me because I can kiss him without standing on my toes. I get butterflies when I look at his gorgeous eyes, strong arms, and his lean and athletic build. I love his black salt-and-pepper hair; it makes him look striking. He has a clean-shaven face and I love how his face feels against mine when we kiss.

When I hear my man's voice it sounds so smooth and when he whispers in my ear I feel loved. I'm appreciative that he is conscientious about his hair, face, and nails. When I lay my head on his chest, I'm intoxicated by his clean, natural scent. What I love about the way he dresses is his handsome look in jeans and a pressed shirt. My Dream Man's overall style is casual, which is comfortable for me. He likes it when I dress casually in jeans and he also likes to see me in skirts or dresses. What he admires about me is my classy, eclectic style.

I fell in love with my Dream Man because his highest values are honesty, integrity, responsibility, trust, compassion, kindness, openness, and forgiveness. One of his deepest beliefs is that we should care for each other and other people, which means a lot to me because I want my life to stand for service and serving others. It's also great that we are both liberal in our political views because I like to lightly debate our perspectives.

He's so inspiring to me with his willingness to be self-aware and take responsibility for his behavior. I truly value that he has great compassion towards others in the world and he always treats me with the greatest respect. It also touches me that he is generous to friends, his family, and to me. One of the things that excites me about him is his curiosity for travel and adventures, which inspires me because I love to travel and go on spontaneous adventures. When he's out in the world, he is open, present, and authentic, which makes me feel comfortable to be with him.

I love his insightful mind because he always has something interesting to talk about. His sense of humor is so hilarious. Every time I hear his heartfelt laugh it brings a smile to my face. I'm proud that my man is incredibly conscious, respectful, and comfortable in his own skin. When I look across the room, I say, "That's my man and I'm so grateful he came into my life." When I sit back and watch him, I truly appreciate his grounded, genuine, and down-to-earth way of being. He's just such a real man. What I love about him is his insatiable curiosity and positive attitude towards life, which is important to me because I am curious and practice a positive outlook.

We spend a lot of our time enjoying each other and laughing. He happens to be a really great handyman, too, and he fixes things for me. He loves outdoor activities as much as I do. We even share the same feelings about animals and he loves dogs, which matters to me because I love my dog and want her to be a part of our activities.

We are compatible in our routine since he is adaptable like me and he enjoys variety in his daily life. It's natural for him to be somewhat active, and he enjoys quiet time. During his own time with others, he enjoys meeting up with a buddy. He cherishes his solo time tinkering with his hobbies, and when he's not doing his own thing I appreciate that he enjoys doing something to make me happy.

My Dream Man is an entrepreneur and he has his financial affairs handled and earns at least $100,000 per year. His work allows him flexibility so that we can freely do things together. I admire that he is dedicated and passionate about his work. His coworkers and colleagues respect that he is inspirational, intelligent, and dedicated to making a difference in the world.

I truly appreciate that he values my expertise and respects my advice. I am grateful that he is flexible with who handles daily life tasks. Our financial arrangement is harmonious since we both contribute financially to our lifestyle needs and future. He is very generous when it comes to spending money on others and me.

I'm pleased that he is conscious about healthy food choices and he also likes to experiment with a variety of foods. At home, my man likes to cook for me since I like to be cooked for and I'll do the dishes. When we go out to eat, he lets me order for myself and he orders the wine. I appreciate his table manners, as they are polite and he takes his time to eat and savor food. When he goes out socially, he is conscious of his drinking limits and is a non-smoker, which is important to me because I am a light drinker and a non-smoker. He is the kind of man who likes to pay for most everything when we go out, but he also is open to my treating him at times.

My man finds me irresistible in that I am authentic, open, and direct with him. What my guy loves about me is my curiosity and positive attitude towards life. He is thoughtful in supporting me in my alone time when I want to tinker in my hobbies, read, or dig in the garden. He appreciates that my spirit is optimistic adventurous and upbeat and he loves my laugh and thinks I'm funny.

He's proud that I am very open-minded, confident, and nonjudgmental. When he speaks about me to others he says that I'm the best thing that ever happened to him, which makes me feel respected, free to be who I am, and unconditionally loved.

My guy encourages me to pursue my dreams by helping me with planning and always being positive. It's natural for him to find creative ways to make me feel special. He shows his romantic side by planning special things for us to do together. He's the kind of man who would surprise me with a trip to Morocco and that makes me appreciate his zest for adventure.

When I walk through the door, he makes me feel adored. In our quiet time together, I know he feels appreciated and confident and he always says I add so much to his life. I know for sure that he makes me feel unconditionally loved.

It gives him blissful pleasure to snuggle, kiss, and hug and out in public he likes to hold hands and walk arm-in-arm. He delights in my body and sees me as a beloved lover and he is attuned to my needs. Physically, what turns him on about me are my eyes, smile, and fit body and most important, he loves and accepts me as I am.

What really worked for me when we first met is that we agreed to just have fun and get to know each other before getting serious. When it comes to making love, we have amazing chemistry and are completely compatible.

My Dream Man is openhearted and willing to connect. When we talk together, his natural way of communicating is agreeable and easy-going. In his style of engaging with me, he is interested in me and is a good conversationalist. We like to talk about spiritual growth, travel, and our relationship and how we can grow and that makes me feel like we're on the same path. As a listener, he knows when to talk and when to listen. When we have a disagreement, we have healthy arguments, but get over them quickly. At times, when I'm angry with him, he says something funny to make me laugh. And when I'm down in the dumps he makes me laugh and cheers me up and I really love him for this.

He's secure and confident and is totally trusting of me. He's a good match for me because I have a self-confident nature and I completely trust him. If I want to spend time alone he lets me be with love and support.

When it comes to material things, what's important to me is that he prefers living a simple life and is comfortable with the basics. When I met my Dream Man he lived near me, which was important because it allowed us to keep our friends and jobs. Our living situation suits us perfectly since we have more than one home and we live in the country and in the city. Our home is our place to create sanctuary. Our interior design and living styles are complementary and easy to blend. We are well-matched in our home care talents, as he likes to cook and I like to do the dishes and he is very handy and can fix anything and I'm happy to let him.

We have many friends from varied backgrounds and lifestyles which contributes to our sense of worldliness. He has children who are grown and not dependent on us and knows that children will not be a part of our relationship. We believe family is important and accept each other's for who they are.

The man of my dreams and I enjoy being outdoors, going to dinner and the movies, visiting art galleries, and taking road trips. When we travel, we enjoy exploring a variety of cultures and countries. My favorite activities while traveling with my man are learning about the history and culture and meeting new people. Traveling with my Dream Man is delightful because he is curious and open to try new things. In looking ahead to our later years, the kind of retirement we envision is traveling the country in an RV.

My Dream Man is spiritual and trusts in a higher power. This pleases me because I believe this is important to the core of our relationship. He believes in the unity of humanity and embraces diversity. Our spiritual lifestyle encompasses attending spiritual events and studying spirituality.

Our relationship is enlivening because we are truly best friends. The most important words to describe the essence of our day-to-day life are laughter, respect, connection, spiritual, joy and love. Our relationship is monogamous and the ultimate fulfillment of our love affair is that we are committed to each other in an adoring relationship.

And we are living a passionate and adventurous life.

Now that you've seen what a full Dream Man story looks like, you can see that there's a very powerful element of dreaming into what's possible for you when you do yours. Don't hesitate to be very specific about what you want. We'll get into the details of how to manifest your Dream Man later. For now just know that you get to have fun with your story, and you get to take the time to really get clear about everything you want in a man and in a relationship.

WHAT ABOUT FANTASY, ROMANCE, MAGIC, AND MYSTERY?

Before you plunge into creating your Dream Man story, I want to take some time to address any potential resistance. I can already sense some of you resisting the process, and that's a normal stage of personal growth. Part of this creation process is allowing your mind to set aside all its logical prowess and encouraging your heart to take over for a while. These are some of the typical questions that women bring up, followed by the short answers, then the longer explanations.

QUESTION: *What happens to the mystery, the excitement, and romance if I pre-design my Dream Man?*

ANSWER: It's still there, he's just easier to spot when he appears.

QUESTION: *Isn't this level of detail a bit contrived and isn't it unrealistic to think I can get everything I want?*

ANSWER: No, clarity is what helps you meet your needs and desires—knowing which things are priorities, which are negotiable and which are not.

QUESTION: *Does this leave the door open for other qualities and possibilities to show up?*

ANSWER: Absolutely—it's an evolving story that will undoubtedly be adjusted as you evolve and discover new qualities as you meet men. But the core values and desires that create your *magnetic resonance* remain constant.

QUESTION: *Will I miss the right guy because I'm only focused on the characteristics and circumstances in my story?*

ANSWER: Not as long as you detach from the outcome and stay open to possibilities—and the magic of surprise. Remember, he's looking for you, too.

QUESTION: *What about allowing magic and attraction to unfold?*

ANSWER: Of course you want your relationship to unfold naturally, but even magic is based on the Law of Attraction.

NEW LENS, MORE MEN

Not only does your Dream Man story leave the door open for the unexpected, it actually expands the possibilities for engaging men through your newly broadened perspective of your needs and dreams. As humans, we tend to see only what we're looking for or what we expect to see, whether it's right for us or not. Your Dream Man story enables you to observe men through a new lens and to have a clearer perception about what really matters to you. This means you'll open your mind to men you may not have previously noticed, or perhaps would have eliminated in the past. Maybe the guy at the office who's been hounding you for a date, but isn't the type you usually go for, will suddenly appear more attractive to you. New men will notice and be drawn to you because your priorities are now internalized and the energy you emanate will be in alignment with your new beliefs and behavior. Your personal clarity will enable you to interact with men more authentically and with a confident sense of empowerment. You can't miss the right guy and he can't miss you, because he'll be attracted to your clear energy and the magnetic resonance that complements what he's looking for in a woman.

NICE FANTASY, WRONG REALITY

Sometimes you may fantasize about a man and a relationship you think you want, but then discover through the dating process that what you thought you wanted actually is no longer compatible with the higher priorities of your life. For example, your Dream Man story may lead you down the path of imagining being with an adventurous, on-the-go man who loves to travel, and yet your highest priorities in your day-to-day life are stability, connecting with community as a couple, and raising a family. Or you may dream of an artistic man who's passionate about his work, but your higher priority is that your man makes a good living. As the saying goes, be careful what you ask for since you might get it. You may also be holding onto an outdated fantasy from your past with some imagined illusion about things you may no longer care about.

BETWEEN YOU AND ME:
Dig Down Deep for What You Really Want

Like many women, for years I thought I wanted to marry a wealthy man to provide me with a secure life. However, after examining my deepest needs and values, I realized that I didn't really need a rich man and actually preferred to contribute to building wealth with my partner. My truest desire was to meet a man who would value my contribution in jointly building an affluent lifestyle. This has proved to be the right approach for me.

Your Dream Man story will make you think about what it will be like to live with your ideal man on a day-to-day basis and what kind of life matches your deepest values. Throughout the process, you'll have an opportunity to make sure you're describing and focusing on attracting an up-to-date version of your Dream Man. The Choose Him Process inspires you to choose what's right for you and to embody the energy that will attract the man of your dreams. You will truly know your priorities, your non-negotiables (not just what you don't want, but what you do want), and where compromise makes sense for you.

THE DIFFERENCE IS IN THE DETAILS

Some women ask: *Won't too many specific details in my story limit my choices?* Trust me, you won't miss the right guy because you're so focused on the details of your story. Details here aren't designed to create an impossible checklist; they're designed to create more clarity and recognition of who is an authentic match. You're looking for compatible energy and resonance—not just physical qualities and external qualifications. In fact, you'll begin to attract men who fit many more of the qualities you desire, but not every man with these qualities is going to be the man of your dreams. You have to kiss a few candidates along the way as you sort through them and move towards the right guy. One of the many gifts of the Choose Him Process is that in the days and weeks ahead, you'll continue to become more and more clear about your priorities and what things no longer hold the importance you once thought they did. Your story will help you discern superficial qualities from your core desires.

Consider walking into your favorite department store to discover that all of the departments throughout the store have been combined into one. Sportswear, dresses, business suits, evening attire, casual clothes, jeans, and lingerie are mixed together on the racks right alongside the men's clothes, appliances, and housewares. You want to find a special outfit for an event and immediately begin to feel overwhelmed. You become frustrated, confused, and disappointed, and ultimately leave the store empty-handed. Think of your Dream Man story as a map that will guide you to the exact rack you're looking for. When you know exactly what you're looking for, it's easier to stay grounded and ignore the frustrations caused by all the things surrounding you that have nothing to do with what you want. But also keep in mind the idea that this map may lead you to more than one perfect fit. It's a navigation tool, but it's not meant to exclude something surprising that jumps out at you along the way. Your feelings and resonance create the attractor factor.

SACREDLY SELFISH TIME

Set time aside—this is your life. I suggest you retreat to a quiet space where you won't be interrupted while you do the activities and create your Dream Man story. It should be a place that feels comfortable, relaxing, and nurturing. This is all about you getting in touch with yourself. As you begin your Dream Man story, allow yourself to indulge in remembering that this process is about YOU and the feelings you want to experience long-term with the man of your dreams. To make sure you're in touch with your true values and desires before you write your story, this first section is all about you. These preliminary personal explorations are designed to get you into a mental space of clarity and inner truth, as well as to open your *feeling center*.

ORIENTATION TO THE CHOOSE HIM PROCESS

Some people like to have a roadmap before they set out on a journey, so here's a quick overview of how the template is organized. The Choose Him Process is designed to take you through multiple aspects of how you envision your Dream Man, but don't forget that it's also about you and about your relationship.

- The Physical
- His Essence
- About Him
- Strictly Business
- About Me
- Our Intimacy
- The Way We Relate
- Our Lifestyle
- Our Spirituality
- The Essence of Our Relationship

When you're done with the whole process, you'll have a story of your Dream Man. This will represent exactly what you want. Then, in Step 3. Attract—Manifest Your Own Ending, you'll learn how to activate your attraction factor.

CAUTION AND A DISCLAIMER

If you're still romantically attached or hung up on someone, it's common to orchestrate your story around *that* man's qualities rather than what you truly want. You won't get the truest version of your story if you're in a compromising frame of mind or are afraid to ask for what you really desire. If you can't create your story from your truth, you're cloning a faulty design.

Next, you're going to be filling in a template that will form the basis for your Dream Man story. The topics and sample statements are designed to trigger your own feelings and values related to the many aspects of your ideal man and relationship. They are not intended to limit you to the possibilities listed. The template is meant to be edited to your own style and language so that it resonates with your deepest feelings. It would be impossible for me to write a template that is universal to all women, so use this as a guide and framework to get you started. Because this process is intended to be a catalyst for your own unique story rather than a comprehensive list of all possibilities, any omission of circumstances, perspectives, or cultural considerations is completely unintentional. I honor and respect the full spectrum of diversity that makes each woman her own special, unique individual.

GUIDELINES

- There is no right answer, just your answer.
- The myriad of ideas and optional responses offered here are intended to inspire you to create your own responses. Customize them and make them as rich and juicy as you want. Feel free to add your own responses, combine options, or leave out the statement completely. He's your man.
- If you find there is some repetition in your responses, that's a clue about what's important to you.

- As you progress through the template, if a statement or topic is not important to you, feel free to leave it out. If you come to a statement that you've already written about in an earlier reply, you can skip ahead or include additional thoughts.
- Trust your heart, not your head.

METHODS FOR RECORDING YOUR DREAM MAN STORY

There are two methods you can choose in moving forward:

1. **WRITE OUT YOUR DREAM MAN STORY BY HAND.** You can simply write your answers in this book and customize them as you go; then rewrite the entire story into a continuous narrative. Even though this might take a bit more time than typing, there are studies that show writing by hand is a right-brain activity that gives you more access to your feelings. Right-brain activity tends to be creative and innovative in character, while left-brain activity is rational and process-oriented.

2. **TYPE YOUR DREAM MAN STORY INTO YOUR COMPUTER.** This is a good option for those of you who might like to read the template and simultaneously type it into your own word processing program—editing, embellishing, and creating your story as you go. Keep in mind that typing is more of a left-brain activity, so do your best to create a comfortable setting and immerse yourself in the feelings of your newly created Dream Man vision.

> **We're proud to announce the online Dream Man Story Creator. If you prefer to use an automated version of the Story Creator template, please visit www.attractingtheloveofmylife.com.**

Whichever option you choose, you'll be well on your way to attracting the man of your dreams right into your life. Be careful not to elaborate too much on each topic. If your story is too long, it can be overwhelming and hard to integrate. Ideally, you will edit and streamline your story to the things that matter most to you.

Remember, you can combine, create your own response, or skip any of the statements. Let the Process begin!

Dream Man STORY CREATOR

Reflect

Create

Attract

THE PHYSICAL

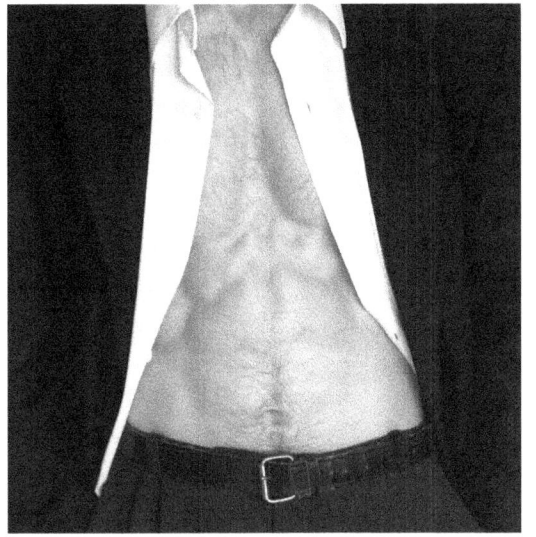

We start with the physical aspect not because it's the most important aspect, but because it's often how we begin a dream. Creating an image of what your Dream Man might look like allows you to envision other aspects of your life together, too. So let's get clear about how your Dream Man inspires your senses. When you think of the physical aspects of your Dream Man, think of all of the details of his appearance, scent, style, and how he takes care of himself—what lights your fire? You'll also be prompted to think about how he feels about you physically, as well as how he makes *you* feel when you're together. Do you want to snuggle up to him or do you want to just admire his physique? Do you want to smell the scent of his neck, play with his hair, or feel his muscles? Your Dream Man's physical body is the body you want to spend time with, adore, and love touching.

Complete the following statements in detail, to the degree that he comes alive in your mind, so you can really feel his physical presence next to yours. Remember, you have total creative license to craft your own ideas. Embellish away.

His Body and Voice

My Dream Man is between _____ and _____ years old since

- *I prefer a younger / an older man*
- *I prefer a man closer to my age*
- *an older man makes me feel younger (more secure, appreciated, etc.)*
- *a younger man makes me feel younger*

_____
_____.

and he is about _____ feet _____ inches tall, which matters to me because _____
_____.

- *I fit nicely under his arm when we're walking together*
- *I love the way a big guy feels*
- *I love the way a man feels who's more my size*
- *I can kiss him without standing on my toes*
- *he's taller than me in my high heels*
- *we can spoon in bed and we fit perfectly*
- *it makes me feel safe and protected*
- *a bigger man makes me feel more feminine*

OR, My Dream Man's looks don't matter so much to me as long as he is *(kind, treats me well, gentle, loving, a free spirit, rich, generous, a great lover, etc.)*

_____
_____
_____
_____
_____
_____.

I get butterflies when I look at his *(handsome face, perfect teeth, smile, gorgeous eyes, full lips, big hands, muscular legs, strong arms, hairy chest, tush, etc.)*

_____
_____
_____
_____
_____
_____.

...and his *(slim, muscular, stocky, medium build, teddy bear like, lean and athletic, chubby in the tummy, etc.)* _____

_____ physique.

I love his *(short, medium, long, thick, slightly balding, brown, black, sandy, red, blonde, salt & pepper, silver)* _____

_____ hair; it makes him look *(sophisticated, contemporary, intelligent, natural, wild, artistic, youthful, striking, gorgeous, exotic, manly, etc.)*

_____

_____

_____.

He has a *(clean-shaven face, sexy mustache, beard, goatee, etc.)* _____

_____ and I love how his face feels against mine when we kiss.

When I hear my man's voice it sounds so *(smooth, melodious, deep, smoky, soothing, sexy, strong, commanding, etc.)* _____...

and when he whispers in my ear I *(just melt, feel calm, feel loved, feel comfortable, feel excited, tingle all over, etc.)* _____.

I'm appreciative that he is *(carefree, casual, conscientious, meticulous, etc.)* _____

_____ about his hair, face, and nails.

When I lay my head on his chest, I'm intoxicated by his *(outdoorsy, beachy, clean, natural, masculine, sexy, musky, etc.)* _____

_____

_____ scent.

Part 4: The Choose Him Process | 81

Appearance and Style

What I love about the way he dresses is his _____

_____.

- athletic and sporty look
- traditional outdoorsman look (Pendleton shirts, vests, etc.)
- casual, relaxed look
- handsome look in jeans and a pressed shirt / T-shirt
- classic look in khakis and a polo
- sophisticated look in business suits or a tux
- unconventional artsy style
- willingness to wear bright colors
- uniform

My Dream Man's overall style is *(steamy sexy, Ivy League, stylish, sophisticated, polished, casual, sporty, rugged, cowboy-like, artistic and carefree, athletic, urban edgy, metrosexual, classic, traditional, etc.)* _____

_____

_____

_____,

which is *(a turn-on, inspiring, comfortable, etc.)* _____

_____

_____ for me.

He likes it when I dress _____
_____ and he also likes to see me _____
_____.

- casually in jeans, khakis, shorts
- in athletic clothes
- short shorts
- in casual business suits
- in skirts or dresses
- in vintage clothes
- in my own artsy, kooky style
- in cocktail and formal attire
- in sexy lingerie
- in nothing at all

What he admires about me is my *(sexy, urban chic, eclectic, trendsetting, fashionable, sophisticated, elegant, classy, delicate and ultra-feminine, natural, cowgirl-like, athletic, tomboyish, etc.)* _____
_____
_____style.

Reach deep into your heart and ask for what you want, not what you may think is possible!

Part 4: The Choose Him Process

HIS ESSENCE

The inner aspects of your Dream Man—his values, beliefs, and life experiences—make up who he is and how he lives in the world. His essence is what drives him when he makes decisions, runs his affairs, and builds his relationships. His essence is what you respect when you get to know who he really is inside, what motivates him, and what he cares about most deeply. This is a core part of your Dream Man story. What kind of man do you want to live and play with, respect, admire, adore, and love?

His Values and Our Values

I fell in love with my Dream Man because his highest values are *(honesty, integrity, loyalty, responsibility, generosity, compassion, trust, collaboration, enthusiasm, kindness, playfulness, security, adventurousness, commitment, learning, openness, sharing, supportiveness, tolerance, forgiveness, etc.)* _____
_____.

One of his deepest beliefs is that _____
_____
_____...

- ♥ *we should live each day to the fullest*
- ♥ *contributing to the community is important*
- ♥ *he has a calling in life and a desire to fulfill it*
- ♥ *curiosity and lifelong learning are an important part of life*
- ♥ *family is the center of life*
- ♥ *contributing to and being involved in our (church, temple, faith, etc.) is a major part of our life*
- ♥ *we should care for each other and other people*

Choose Him

... which means a lot to me because (your own answer) _____

_____

_____

_____

_____.

It's also great that we _____

_____

_____...

- ♥ *share common political perspectives*
- ♥ *are both (liberal, conservative, independent, green) in our political views*
- ♥ *are comfortable having diverse political views*
- ♥ *don't really care about politics*

...because I like to *(have amicable discussions about current affairs, be on the same page about issues, lightly debate our perspectives, debate our perspectives, talk about more meaningful topics, etc.)* _____

_____

_____

_____.

How He Treats Himself, Me, and Others

He's so inspiring to me with his willingness to _____
_____
_____
_____
_____
_____
_____.

- ♥ *work on improving himself*
- ♥ *ask for help when he needs it*
- ♥ *be self-sufficient and take care of himself*
- ♥ *be self-aware and take responsibility for his behavior*
- ♥ *take care of business*
- ♥ *tell the clear and simple truth*
- ♥ *be receptive to kind advice*

I truly value that he _____
_____
_____
_____.

- ♥ *walks his talk in how he treats others*
- ♥ *has great compassion towards others in the world*
- ♥ *is responsible and keeps his word and commitments*
- ♥ *always tries to do the right thing*
- ♥ *is truly a nice guy to everyone*

... and he always (*supports my dreams, speaks positively about me to others, treats me with the greatest respect, etc.*) _____
_____.

It also touches me that he is _____
_____.

- *generous with his time*
- *generous and kind of heart*
- *generous to friends, his family, and me*
- *generous to specific causes that are important and meaningful to him*
- *philanthropic and a true humanitarian*

His Manner and His Mind

One of the things that excites me about him is _____
_____
_____ ...

- 💜 *that he is comfortable in a board room or a pool hall*
- 💜 *his drive and ambition*
- 💜 *his energy and passion for his work*
- 💜 *his passion for (sports, cars, motorcycles, flying, skiing, art, etc.)*
- 💜 *his curiosity for travel and adventures*
- 💜 *his commitment to community life (politics, service, church, etc.)*
- 💜 *his closeness to his family*

...which *(impresses, intrigues, inspires, amazes, impacts, etc.)* me because *(your own answer)* _____
_____
_____.

When he's out in the world, he is _____
_____ ...

- 💜 *powerfully present*
- 💜 *large and in charge*
- 💜 *balanced and independent*
- 💜 *open, present, and authentic*
- 💜 *reserved and observant*
- 💜 *confident and secure*

...which makes me feel *(your own answer)* _____
_____
_____.

I love his *(quick, witty, inquisitive, analytical, creative, well-read, intelligent, rational, insightful, etc.)*
_____
_____
_____
mind because he _____
_____.

- ♥ *keeps me on my toes*
- ♥ *always has something interesting to talk about*
- ♥ *is an avid reader and it's a lifelong passion of mine*
- ♥ *enjoys learning new things*
- ♥ *enjoys teaching me new things*
- ♥ *knows so much about so many things*

His sense of humor _____
_____
_____
_____.

- ♥ *makes me laugh out loud*
- ♥ *makes me not take life so seriously*

- ♥ *is always positive and makes me feel better*
- ♥ *is so hilarious*
- ♥ *is subtle and droll*
- ♥ *engages others in a positive way*

Every time I hear his *(joyful, jubilant, exuberant, jovial, infectious, spirited, belly, heartfelt, hardy, animated, cheerful, etc.)* _____
_____ laugh it brings a smile to my face.

Part 4: The Choose Him Process

I'm proud that my man is incredibly *(conscious, creative, open-minded, sensitive, powerful, non-judgmental, spontaneous, comfortable in his own skin, kind, private, respectful, unselfish, loyal, honorable, generous, etc.)* _____
_____
_____.

When I look across the room, I say, 'That's my man and _____
_____
_____
_____."

- ♥ *I'm so grateful he came into my life*
- ♥ *I admire how he wins people over*
- ♥ *I appreciate how he likes and respects himself*
- ♥ *I marvel at how he maneuvers in the world*
- ♥ *I'm so proud to be with him*

When I sit back and watch him, I truly appreciate his *(happy go-lucky, playful, adventurous, artistic, down-to-earth, charismatic, warm-hearted, grounded, secure, sensitive, caring, genuine, confident, quiet, contemplative, etc.)* _____
_____
_____
_____
_____
_____way of being.

He's just *(amazing, a wonderful man, a great guy, so sexy, such a real man, etc.)* _____
_____.

His Energy

What I love about him is his _____

_____

_____...

- *abundant energy and vitality*
- *energetic and fun-loving spirit*
- *insatiable curiosity and positive attitude towards life*
- *easy-going nature*
- *mellow, laid-back attitude*
- *drive and ambition*

...which is important to me because *(your own answer)*

_____
_____
_____
_____
_____
_____
_____.

> *This is a good place to take a breather. It takes some time and thought to focus on what you really want. You will feel very satisfied, and that the effort was well worth finally having a clear and detailed vision of your ideal guy.*

Part 4: The Choose Him Process

ABOUT HIM

Beyond his essence is his natural way of being in the world. What type of person is he? What's he like when he goes out socially? What is his daily rhythm? What kind of food does he like? What's he really good at? In this section, explore who he is and what you love about him. In the end, you will have a clear idea of what type of Dream Man you want to find.

With Me

We spend a lot of our time _____
_____
_____
_____
_____
_____ .

- ♥ *enjoying each other and laughing a lot*
- ♥ *meeting new people*
- ♥ *people watching*
- ♥ *dancing*
- ♥ *playing sports (golf, tennis, volleyball, skiing, etc.)*
- ♥ *doing things outdoors*
- ♥ *watching TV and movies together*
- ♥ *meditating or doing other spiritual practices*
- ♥ *reading to each other, discussing ideas*
- ♥ *making love*

He happens to be a really great *(dancer, artist, athlete, singer, sailor, skier, musician, poet, outdoors man, handyman, etc.)* _____, too, and he _____ _____ _____ _____.

- ♥ *takes me dancing often*
- ♥ *invites me to join him in athletic activities*
- ♥ *sings to me often*
- ♥ *takes me sailing (camping, to sporting events, galleries, theater, etc.)*
- ♥ *loves it when I go skiing (hiking, biking, boating, etc.) with him*
- ♥ *plays his (piano, guitar, etc.) for me*
- ♥ *reads poetry to me often*
- ♥ *invites me along on his outdoor adventures*
- ♥ *fixes things for me*
- ♥ *takes care of repairing things around the house*

He loves *(sex, making love, golf, sports, reading, art, music, movies, plays, outdoor activities, etc.)* _____ _____ as much as I do.

We even share the same feelings about animals and *(he loves dogs, he loves cats, he loves all animals, we agree not to have animals, etc.)* _____ _____ _____, which matters to me because *(your own answer)* _____ _____.

His Time

We are compatible in our daily routine since he is *(a night owl, a morning person, a mid-day person, adaptable etc.)* _____ like me, and he _____ .

- ♥ *is happy to have a comfortable, consistent routine*
- ♥ *is very flexible and willing to change his routine*
- ♥ *enjoys variety in his daily life*
- ♥ *wants a routine he can count on*

It's natural for him to be _____
_____
_____ .

- ♥ *extremely active and always doing something*
- ♥ *very active, but he also likes some mellow time*
- ♥ *somewhat active, and he enjoys quiet time*
- ♥ *a true homebody who appreciates relaxing*

During his own time with others, he enjoys _____
_____
_____
_____
_____
_____
_____ .

- ♥ *having genuine friends over to hang out*
- ♥ *volunteering in the community*   *(more options →)*

- ♥ *attending cultural events*
- ♥ *going to sporting events*
- ♥ *playing sports and games*
- ♥ *hanging out in the local coffee shop (pub, library, bookstore, park, etc.)*
- ♥ *meeting up with a buddy*

He cherishes his solo time *(relaxing, reading, watching TV, playing an instrument, listening to music, spending time outdoors, playing a solo sport, tinkering with his hobbies, working out, etc.)* _____

_____

_____

and when he's not doing his own thing, I appreciate that he *(checks to see what I want to do, enjoys doing something to make me happy, gives me the same space whenever I need it)* _____

_____

_____ …

> *This template is meant to be a catalyst for your own thoughts and feelings. Feel free to create your own answers.*

His Food Attitudes and Social Etiquette

I'm pleased that he _____
_____
_____ ...

- ♥ *is a vegetarian / vegan*
- ♥ *is a meat and potatoes man*
- ♥ *prefers healthy and organic foods*
- ♥ *is conscious about healthy food choices*
- ♥ *prefers his cultural food*
- ♥ *enjoys many ethnic dishes*

...and he also _____
_____
_____.

- ♥ *is open to trying new foods*
- ♥ *likes to experiment with a variety of foods*
- ♥ *is happy with basic foods*
- ♥ *is a real foodie and loves to eat out*

At home, my man likes to _____
_____
_____
_____ ...

- ♥ *cook for me*
- ♥ *have me cook for him*
- ♥ *share in cooking together*   *(more options →)*

96 Choose Him

- ♥ take turns cooking
- ♥ cook for others (entertain)
- ♥ have someone cook for us
- ♥ order takeout (delivery)

...since *(your own answer)* _____
_____.

When we go out to eat, he *(orders for me, lets me order for myself, orders the wine for us, lets me order the wine, etc.)* _____
_____
_____.

I appreciate his table manners, as they are *(impeccable, polite, traditional, proper, elegant, not fussy, common sense, etc.)* _____
_____
_____ and he _____
_____
_____.

- ♥ uses his utensils in the proper way
- ♥ follows formal table etiquette
- ♥ has casual table manners
- ♥ chews his food politely
- ♥ takes his time to eat and savor food
- ♥ relishes food with gusto

When he goes out socially, he _____
_____and_____ ...

- ♥ is a non-drinker
- ♥ is conscious of his drinking limits
- ♥ is fun and enjoys drinking
- ♥ avoids recreational drugs
- ♥ is conscious of his limits with recreational drugs
- ♥ is a party guy who enjoys recreational drugs
- ♥ is a non-smoker
- ♥ occasionally smokes
- ♥ enjoys smoking as much as I do

...which is important to me because *(your own answer)* _____
_____
_____.

He is the kind of man who _____
_____
_____.

- ♥ insists on paying for everything when we go out together
- ♥ likes to pay for most everything when we go out, but he also is open to my treating him at times
- ♥ likes the fact that I'm always considerate in paying my share
- ♥ likes it that we take turns treating
- ♥ is secure in himself and appreciates that I am well-off and can afford to pay for everything
- ♥ appreciates a financially secure and generous woman

Next, put your attention on you, because you deserve to have everything you want.

STRICTLY BUSINESS

All of the lovey-dovey stuff is wonderful, but when some of the fairy dust dissipates, you're left with the details of life: work, finances, and schedules. What is your ideal life with your Dream Man? Make it work for you.

What He Does

My Dream Man is *(an entrepreneur, a professional, a business man, an educator, in the creative arts, in the healing arts, in public life, retired, etc.)* _____

_____

_____,

and he _____ .

- ♥ *earns at least $ _____ per year*
- ♥ *has his financial affairs handled*
- ♥ *is financially stable and secure*
- ♥ *is wealthy from previous ventures and now pursues other interests*
- ♥ *is very wealthy and successful in his career*
- ♥ *is happy with his work and I'm comfortable with whatever he earns*

His pursuits allow him _____

_____

_____

_____

_____ .

(options →)

- *a predictable schedule (so that I know when to expect him home, so that we can plan vacations, etc.)*
- *to work 9-to-5 weekdays (and be home for dinner most every night, and be home on the weekends to be with the family, etc.)*
- *to not mind long hours (because my work is demanding too, etc.)*
- *to travel (and I enjoy going along and that gives me time to myself, etc.)*
- *flexibility (so that we can freely do things together, because I have a hectic schedule, because I travel with my work etc.)*

I admire that he _____
_____
_____
_____
_____
_____.

- *is dedicated and passionate about his work (retirement, craft, talent, etc.)*
- *has achieved a level of respect/recognition/prestige in his field*
- *is fulfilled in his career and wants to grow professionally*
- *is fulfilled with his work, but flexible and open to change*
- *is comfortable and secure in his work*
- *is truly enjoying his retirement*

His coworkers and colleagues respect that he is *(a solid man, reliable, a great guy, responsible, a leader, a visionary, inspirational, creative, talented, gifted, dedicated to helping others, intelligent and successful, a global and dynamic thinker, dedicated to making a difference in the world, etc.)*
_____
_____
_____.

Finances and Roles

I truly appreciate that he _____
_____
_____
_____
_____ .

- ♥ thinks highly of my work and respects my dedication
- ♥ understands the demands of my work
- ♥ is proud of me and my accomplishments
- ♥ values my expertise and respects my advice
- ♥ treasures all that I do for our family life
- ♥ fully supports me being a stay-at-home mom

I'm grateful that he _____
_____
_____
_____
_____
_____ .

- ♥ helps me balance work and our time together
- ♥ is in the same industry as me / is in a different industry than me
- ♥ is flexible with who handles daily life tasks (cooks, shops, laundry, etc.)
- ♥ loves that I take care of most everything around the house
- ♥ prefers that I'm home so that we can spend more time together
- ♥ takes responsibility for our financial needs so that I can fulfill my dreams

Our financial arrangement is harmonious since _____
_____
_____
_____
_____
_____.

- ♥ *he's prudent with handling money and invests well for our future*
- ♥ *he earns enough money so that we can live a comfortable lifestyle*
- ♥ *he's wealthy and we live an extraordinary lifestyle*
- ♥ *he is open to my being the primary breadwinner (he's a stay-at-home father, artist, retired, etc.)*
- ♥ *we don't consider money an issue*
- ♥ *we share in building our wealth and security*
- ♥ *we both contribute financially to our lifestyle needs and future*

He is _____
_____
_____
_____
_____.

- ♥ *very generous when it comes to spending money on others and me*
- ♥ *generous with me, but sensible about how he spends money*
- ♥ *thoughtful about how he spends money and always ensures I have what I need*
- ♥ *mindful in how he spends money and is attentive to our financial security*
- ♥ *respectful of my independence in spending the money I earn, and we share household expenses*
- ♥ *happy when I spend money on him and his ego stays in tact*

ABOUT ME

The man of your dreams is the man who makes you feel your absolute best. He's the man who treats you as you want to be treated—he is a reflection of you in many ways. You become more of who you are when you're with him, and he allows you to live out your true potential.

My Personality

My man finds me irresistible in that _____

_____

_____.

- *I let him pursue me and he still does*
- *I made him want to be a better man and he is*
- *I was comfortable with showing him how much I care*
- *I freely express my needs and standards for our relationship*
- *I am authentic, open, and direct with him*
- *I am very attractive (sexy, fascinating, mysterious, etc.)*
- *I'm so much fun to be with*

What my guy loves about me is my _____

_____.

- *abundant energy and vitality*
- *energetic and fun-loving spirit*
- *outgoing personality*
- *curiosity and positive attitude towards life*
- *drive and ambition for success*
- *easy-going nature*

(more options →)

Part 4: The Choose Him Process | 103

- *caring and nurturing qualities*
- *creative and artistic nature*
- *sensitivity and intuitive nature*

He is thoughtful in supporting me in my alone time when I want to *(relax, read, write, explore the internet, watch movies, play an instrument, listen to music, talk on the phone, create art, tinker in my hobbies, work out at the gym, lounge by the pool, dig in the garden, etc.)* _____

_____

_____

_____.

He appreciates that my spirit is *(optimistic, upbeat, enthusiastic, playful, adventurous, mischievous, open, laid-back, peaceful, mellow, reserved, etc.)* _____

_____

and _____

_____.

- *my sense of humor is magnified around him*
- *he thinks I'm hilarious and a laugh a minute*
- *he's attracted to my dry sense of humor*
- *he loves my laugh and thinks I'm funny*
- *we laugh at the same things*

His Love for Me

He's proud that I am very *(conscious, confident, creative, open-minded, powerful, non-judgmental, kind, generous, spontaneous, comfortable in my own skin, respectful, unselfish, loyal, honorable, classy, etc.)*

_____.

When he speaks about me to others he says that

_____

_____ ...

- ♥ *I'm the best thing that ever happened to him*
- ♥ *he's the luckiest guy in the world*
- ♥ *I'm original and fascinating*
- ♥ *I'm intelligent and intuitive*
- ♥ *I'm his best friend*
- ♥ *I have a great sense of humor*
- ♥ *I'm witty and a lot of fun*
- ♥ *I'm comfortable with who I am*
- ♥ *I'm down to earth*

...which makes me feel *(honored, adored, cherished, respected, admired, unconditionally loved, free to be who I am, that he has my highest good in mind, held on a pedestal, etc.)* _____

_____

_____.

OUR INTIMACY

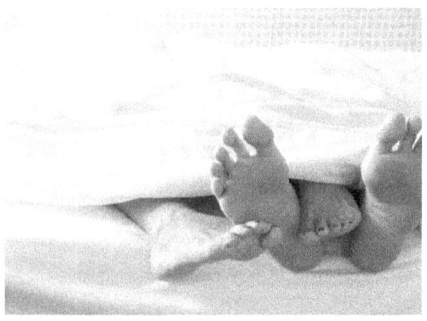

When the two of you are alone, what is it that you want to experience most with him? Intimacy includes everything from talking and touching to sex. It's the experience you have with him and with yourself that brings you closer together, allows you to be vulnerable, and cements your relationship connection. When you're out in public, how do you want him to treat you?

My Needs

My guy encourages me to pursue my dreams by *(sharing his ideas, giving me thoughtful feedback, helping me with planning, cheering me on, participating in them, always being positive, etc.)*

_____
_____.

It's natural for him to _____

_____
_____
_____
_____.

- ♥ *compliment me a lot*
- ♥ *want to build my confidence*
- ♥ *pamper me and be aware of my needs by bringing me coffee in the morning (making me breakfast in bed, always checking in with me to see what I need, etc.)*
- ♥ *find creative ways to make me feel special*

He shows his romantic side by _____

_____.

(options →)

106 Choose Him

- *bringing me flowers for no special occasion*
- *calling me just to say "hi" and see how my day is going*
- *always remembering my birthday, Valentine's day, and our anniversary*
- *opening doors for me and being a true gentleman*
- *always telling me how much he loves me and how happy he is to be with me*
- *always giving me affectionate pecks, pats, and squeezes*
- *telling me often that he thinks I'm beautiful and wonderful*
- *scattering love notes around the house*
- *planning special things for us to do together (trips, theater, dinner, etc.)*
- *getting teary-eyed watching a love story*
- *sharing his deepest feelings about my importance in his life*

He's the kind of man who would _____

_____

_____

_____ ...

- *surprise me with a weekend getaway*
- *surprise me with a trip to Paris (Morocco, Thailand, etc.)*
- *surprise me with beautiful jewelry or perfume*
- *take me shopping and patiently watch me try on clothes*
- *surprise me with a new tennis racquet, bike, etc.*
- *surprise me with a gourmet meal he prepared himself*
- *surprise me with flowers*
- *go to chick flicks with me to make me happy*
- *get out of bed to buy me ice cream or champagne*
- *arrange a gathering or surprise party with my friends*
- *hang out with my girlfriends and me and have a blast*

...and that makes me *(your own answer)* _____
_____
_____.

When I walk through the door, he makes me feel *(missed, adored, beautiful, sexy, smart, cherished, important in his life, etc.)* _____
_____
_____
_____.

In our quiet time together, I know he feels *(fulfilled, proud, appreciated, valued, manly, loved, admired, like my hero, grateful, confident, supported, etc.)* _____
_____,

and he always says _____
_____
_____
_____
_____
_____.

- ♥ *I add so much to his life*
- ♥ *I'm never boring and I'm one of a kind*
- ♥ *he loves the warm and comfortable home I create*
- ♥ *I'm an amazing woman*
- ♥ *I give him peace of mind*
- ♥ *that he loves and respects me as I am*   *(more options →)*

- *I'm the one he wants to be with forever*
- *he can talk to me about anything*
- *we're just so comfortable together*
- *we're true soul mates / spiritual partners*

I know for sure that he makes me feel *(desirable, special, protected, safe and cared for, I can really trust him, beautiful, unconditionally loved, cherished, as if anything is possible, etc.)* _____
_____
_____
_____
_____
_____
_____
_____
_____.

Physically Speaking

It gives him blissful pleasure to_____
_____...

- ♥ *snuggle, kiss, and hug*
- ♥ *just hold me*
- ♥ *give me a massage*
- ♥ *show his affection in many ways*
- ♥ *hold my hand while we're watching TV*

... and out in public he _____
_____.

- ♥ *likes to hold hands and walk arm-in-arm*
- ♥ *likes to touch and is very affectionate*
- ♥ *prefers to save his affection for private moments*
- ♥ *shows affection with loving looks and smiles*

He delights in my body and sees me as *(a goddess, a seductress, a beloved lover, sensual and feminine, sexy and voluptuous, etc.)*
_____
_____
_____
_____ ...

...and he is *(a super hot kisser, gentle, sensitive, attuned to my needs, romantic and tender, a fantastic lover, sensual and sizzling, etc.)* _____
_____
_____.

Physically, what turns him on about me are my *(eyes, lips, smile, legs, fit body, curvaceous body, voluptuous body, petite body, statuesque body, etc.)* _____ and_____ and most importantly he loves and accepts me as I am.

What really worked for me when we first met is that:

- we agreed to just have fun and get to know each other before getting serious
- we both wanted to become friends before having sex (making love)
- we both felt free to express ourselves sexually without constraint or rules
- he accepted my decision to hold off on sex until we had a committed relationship
- we agreed to reserve our intimate passion for marriage

When it comes to making love, we *(love to linger in bed, have amazing chemistry, are adventurous and experimental, make it a high/low priority, are passionate and romantic, spontaneous, have lots of foreplay, prefer to just cuddle, can take it or leave it. etc.)* _____ _____ _____, _____ and we are completely compatible.

THE WAY WE RELATE

Imagine the type of communication and care you'd like to have with your Dream Man. Does he like to talk with you into the wee hours of the night? Does he like to listen to your dreams? Does he disagree with you with kind words? Does he take care of you when you're down?

Talking

My Dream Man is *(caring, thoughtful, considerate, supportive, emotionally available, open-hearted, willing to connect, a great communicator, engaging, etc.)* _____
_____.

When we talk together, his natural way of communicating is
_____
_____.

- ♥ *honest and candid*
- ♥ *agreeable and easy-going*
- ♥ *gentle with criticism*
- ♥ *open to constructive criticism*
- ♥ *open to learning and challenging each other*
- ♥ *debating his point but is willing to change his mind*
- ♥ *willing to sit down and talk things through*
- ♥ *a man of few words who listens more than he speaks*

In his style of engaging with me, he _____
_____.

- 💜 *is interested in me and is a good conversationalist*
- 💜 *is curious to know more about my world*
- 💜 *intellectually and emotionally piques my interest*
- 💜 *is present—when he's there, he's really there for me and about me*
- 💜 *is more reserved and the strong quiet type*
- 💜 *likes to talk more than most men*
- 💜 *communicates with me on every level*
- 💜 *makes himself available when I really need to talk*
- 💜 *is willing to share his deepest feelings, even his fears*

We like to talk about *(business ideas, setting life goals, spiritual growth, current events, politics, travel, vacation plans, our kids' lives and family activities, entertaining, movies, home improvement, the meaning of life, our relationship and how we can grow, etc.)*

_____
_____
_____
_____
_____,

and that makes me feel *(like we're truly connected, like we're true partners, that we're on the same wavelength, that we're on the same path, that he respects my opinion, etc.)* _____
_____
_____.

Listening

As a listener, he _____
_____
_____
_____
_____.

- ♥ *knows when to talk and when to listen*
- ♥ *is a great sounding board without trying to fix the problem*
- ♥ *hears what I'm saying and gives good feedback / engages me further*
- ♥ *enjoys hearing about my daily activities, thoughts, and opinions*
- ♥ *is so tuned in to me and he picks up on the smallest details*
- ♥ *listens to me without making me feel foolish about my thoughts and ideas*

Differing

When we have a disagreement, we _____
_____
_____.

- ♥ *argue passionately and make up just as passionately*
- ♥ *have healthy arguments, but get over them quickly*
- ♥ *are able to argue respectfully*
- ♥ *never argue, but we have respectful discussions*
- ♥ *listen to each other's points of view before responding*
- ♥ *resolve it before going to bed*
- ♥ *avoid calling each other hurtful names*
- ♥ *both want to actively, rationally resolve our conflicts*

At times, when I'm angry with him, he _____
_____
_____
_____
_____
_____ .

- 💜 *knows when to leave me alone so I can work it through privately*
- 💜 *hugs me and apologizes*
- 💜 *says something funny to make me laugh*
- 💜 *respectfully asks that I sit down and talk to him*
- 💜 *listens and reacts rationally*

And when I'm down in the dumps _____
_____
_____ …

- 💜 *he is kind and gentle*
- 💜 *he gives me space to allow me to work through my own feelings*
- 💜 *shows he cares and checks in on me without hovering*
- 💜 *he hugs and cuddles me and let's me know everything will be okay*
- 💜 *he makes me laugh and cheers me up*

…and I really love him for this.

Being

He is _____.

- ♥ secure and confident and is totally trusting of me
- ♥ just jealous enough to make me feel special
- ♥ secure and confident, but is protective of me
- ♥ a little possessive and protective of me

He's a good match for me because _____
_____
_____.

- ♥ I have a confident nature and I completely trust him
- ♥ I'm a little jealous, because he is so special
- ♥ he makes me feel loved and safe
- ♥ I know he'll always stand up for me

If I _____
_____
_____ …

- ♥ want to go out with my friends
- ♥ want to go shopping
- ♥ want to spend time alone
- ♥ want to take a vacation by myself
- ♥ want to spend time working

...he _____
_____
_____
_____
_____
_____
_____
_____.

- ♥ sends me off and encourages me to have a great time
- ♥ lets me be without questioning or hovering
- ♥ helps me plan my trip and sends me off with a kiss
- ♥ lets me be with love and support
- ♥ has things he likes to do without me
- ♥ misses me but understands my need for personal time and space

> *Now he's beginning to feel real and like a part of your life.*

OUR LIFESTYLE

Everything and everyone around you makes your relationship complete. Your lifestyle includes your home, family, children, friends, and what you do for fun and leisure. What kind of full and complete life do you want to live with your mate? Do you want kids? Do you want to travel? Do you want a home where you can entertain family and friends? Your lifestyle is the life you create with the outside world, too. What's yours?

In the World at Large

When it comes to material things, what's important to me is that he prefers _____
_____
_____.

- ♥ *living a simple life and is comfortable with the basics*
- ♥ *the comforts of a traditional lifestyle*
- ♥ *a well-to-do life with recreational toys, the latest technology, cars, sports equipment, etc.*
- ♥ *the finer things in life and enjoys fine wine, art, and a cultural life, etc.*
- ♥ *the very best of everything: a vacation home or two, exotic first class travel, etc.*

Home

When I met my Dream Man, he _____
_____
_____.

- ♥ *was grateful that I would move across the country to be with him*
- ♥ *was willing to follow me wherever I go (since I travel a lot, get transferred often, etc.)*

(more options →)

118 | Choose Him

- *lived near me, which meant we could (keep our friends/activities, be near family, keep our jobs, etc.)*
- *liked that we live apart in our own homes (so that we have our own time and space, have diversity in our lives, etc.)*

Our living situation suits us perfectly, since we _____

_____

_____

_____…

- *share his beautiful home*
- *share my beautiful home*
- *share our new home*
- *have more than one home*

…and we live *(in the city, in the country, in the suburbs, at the beach, on a ranch, in the mountains, on a boat, in an RV, etc.)* _____

_____

_____.

Our primary home is our place _____

_____.

- *to create sanctuary*
- *to relax and retreat*
- *to entertain with friends and family*
- *to enjoy social events and cultural activities*
- *to have fun with our hobbies*
- *to raise our children*
- *to play and chill out*
- *to work, since I work from home*
- *to each have our individual way of life and space to ourselves*

Our interior design and living styles are _____
_____
_____
_____.

- ♥ *completely compatible*
- ♥ *complementary and easy to blend*
- ♥ *left up to me to manage*
- ♥ *left up to him to manage*
- ♥ *left up to each other to manage for our own homes*
- ♥ *merged and coordinated with an interior designer*
- ♥ *easy-going and not that important*

We are well matched in our home care talents, since_____
_____
_____
_____.

- ♥ *he likes to cook and I like to do the dishes*
- ♥ *I like to cook and he likes to do the dishes*
- ♥ *we like to cook and do the dishes together*
- ♥ *I take care of the inside of the house and he takes care of the outside*
- ♥ *we share in household chores*
- ♥ *he is very considerate in sharing space*
- ♥ *he is very handy and can fix anything and I'm happy to let him*
- ♥ *we both enjoy home improvement projects*
- ♥ *we both love to garden and care for our property*
- ♥ *we agree to hire house care help*
- ♥ *we both take care of our own places*

Friends and Family

We _____
_____
_____ ...

- 💜 each have a lot of friends
- 💜 embrace each other's friends and accept them for who they are
- 💜 prefer to keep our friends separate
- 💜 have many friends from varied backgrounds and lifestyles
- 💜 include each other's friends in our activities
- 💜 are both more private and prefer just a few close friends

...which contributes to our sense of *(enriching our life, connection, independence, autonomy, freedom, being social, diversity, worldliness, variety, etc.)* _____
_____.

He _____
_____
_____
_____ ...

- 💜 has children
- 💜 has children in his care and wants more
- 💜 has no kids but wants to someday
- 💜 has no children and no plans to have any
- 💜 has children who are grown and not dependent on us

and_____

_____.

- 💜 *loves kids and wants them as part of his life*
- 💜 *accepts my kids and lovingly joins my family*
- 💜 *respects my desire not to have children*
- 💜 *prefers that children are not part of our lives*
- 💜 *accepts that children will not be a part of our relationship*

We believe _____

_____.

- 💜 *family is important and accept each other's for who they are*
- 💜 *family is everything and we will do whatever it takes to be close to them and care for them*
- 💜 *in living our own lives and spending limited time with family*
- 💜 *in respecting each other's boundaries with family*
- 💜 *in living a far distance from our families*

Out and About

The man of my dreams and I enjoy_____

_____

_____.

- 💜 *window shopping*
- 💜 *going to sporting events*
- 💜 *being outdoors and hiking (skiing, running, roaming in parks, etc.)*
- 💜 *sharing in a hobby (horses, gardening, painting, etc.)*
- 💜 *going out to dinner and a movie*
- 💜 *visiting and socializing with friends (family, co-workers, clients)*

(more options →)

- *listening to music*
- *going dancing*
- *going gambling (horse races, casinos)*
- *going wine tasting*
- *taking road trips*
- *visiting art galleries, museums, and cultural events*

(The list is endless.)

When we travel, we enjoy _____
_____
_____
_____
_____.

- *exploring a variety of cultures and countries*
- *roaming the U.S. in an RV*
- *lounging on the beach in tropical climates*
- *going on adventure trips*
- *yachting in exotic places*
- *camping under the stars*
- *five-star trips (Orient Express, Abercrombie & Fitch safaris, etc.)*
- *escaping to romantic hideaways*

My favorite activities while traveling with my man are _____

_____.

- 💜 *sightseeing*
- 💜 *trying new cuisines*
- 💜 *learning about the history and culture*
- 💜 *trying a new activity or challenge (skydiving, motorcycling, deep sea diving, etc.)*
- 💜 *touring museums*
- 💜 *shopping (for artifacts, clothes, art, etc.)*
- 💜 *being pampered in spas*
- 💜 *meeting new people*
- 💜 *hanging out with the locals*

Traveling with my Dream Man is delightful because he_____

_____.

- 💜 *likes the same things I do*
- 💜 *is comfortable doing separate things at times*
- 💜 *takes care of me and leads the way*
- 💜 *lets me lead the way*
- 💜 *is curious and open to try new things*
- 💜 *loves our special time together*

Our Future Lifestyle

In looking ahead to our later years, the kind of retirement we envision is _____
_____.

- *continuing to remain active in our work*
- *being able to stop working while we're young*
- *kicking back at home with hobbies*
- *remaining active in community affairs*
- *traveling the country in an RV*
- *becoming snowbirds and chasing the sun*
- *making our lives about the grandkids*

OUR SPIRITUALITY

Inside of your heart is a spiritual desire. What kind of man matches that desire? What sort of actions in the world demonstrate who he is deep in his heart? No matter what your spiritual preferences are, do you want a man who journeys on the same path with you, or one who brings a different perspective? The choice is yours.

My Dream Man _____
_____
_____
_____.

- *is spiritual and trusts in a higher power*
- *believes in God (a higher power, Allah, etc.), but does not attend organized services*
- *has strong religious faith and attends organized services (church, temple, prayer, etc.) regularly*
- *has his own spiritual practices (meditation, yoga, ritual, etc.)*
- *has no spiritual or religious beliefs and we share agnostic/atheist perspectives*

This pleases me because I *(share the same beliefs, look forward to sharing our faith, believe this is important to the core of our relationship, want us to grow spiritually together, am not connected to any spiritual beliefs, etc.)* _____
_____.

He believes _____
_____.

- that strong faith in a higher power (God, Allah, Shangdi, Adi-buddha, etc.) is the key to healing humanity
- our (religious, sacred, holy, spiritual, etc) faith and devotion can get us through anything
- in the unity of humanity and embraces diversity
- that we should share resources and build community
- in being compassionate and charitable towards others
- that people are responsible for themselves and create their own destinies
- in our free will, existence, and karma

Our spiritual lifestyle encompasses _____
_____
_____.

- creating and evolving our world together
- attending spiritual events and studying spirituality
- sharing our spiritual practices (yoga, meditation, ritual, etc.)
- praying together often (regularly, daily)
- participating in (church, temple, community) activities
- sharing the differences in our beliefs
- spending time in nature
- travel to foreign sacred sites
- just being good people while on this earth

THE ESSENCE OF OUR RELATIONSHIP

So far, you've created a vision for quite an amazing Dream Man, but you're not done yet. This might be a good time to make another cup of tea or get up and stretch. You want to feel totally content during this part. The last aspect of your Dream Man is the essence, true feelings, and experiences you have with this perfect partner. What is your relationship like? What is your relationship like as it grows? What is the ultimate fulfillment of your union with this man? Dream big, as you are about to see him come into your life.

Our relationship is enlivening because we _____
_____
_____
_____
_____ .

- ♥ *challenge and encourage each other to live our fullest potential*
- ♥ *complement each other in our uniqueness, creativity, and energy*
- ♥ *are soul-connected partners on a common path*
- ♥ *are so much alike and interested in similar things*
- ♥ *have clear roles and appreciate how we both contribute*
- ♥ *are truly best friends*
- ♥ *allow each other independence and freedom to also live our individual lives*

The most important words to describe the essence of our day-to-day life are *(laughter, harmony, contentment, passion, excitement, support, respect, connection, affection, stimulating, spiritual, sharing, satisfaction, peace, joy, love, attentiveness, etc.)* _____
_____ , _____ ,
and _____ .

Our relationship is *(committed, monogamous, faithful, open to alternative partners, etc.)* _____
_____
_____ ,

and the ultimate fulfillment of our love affair is that we are _____
_____
_____ .

- ♥ *married and are raising a family*
- ♥ *married and have children in our lives*
- ♥ *married and enjoying our independence/empty nest*
- ♥ *committed to each other in an equal partnership*
- ♥ *committed to each other in an adoring partnership*
- ♥ *committed to each other and living separately*

Your Evolving Ever After

And we are living _____
_____
_____ .

- ♥ *authentically ever after . . . the beginning*
- ♥ *joyfully and harmoniously, and will forever*
- ♥ *a mutually fulfilling life together*
- ♥ *a passionate and adventurous life*
- ♥ *create your own*

CONGRATULATIONS! The thrilling part is still to come after you've written out your full story and read it, which begins to change your magnetic resonance and ignites the Law of Attraction.

WRITE YOUR OWN STORY

To complete your story, write or type each entire statement and your answers to form one continuous narrative. Writing the entire narrative into a unified story is essential to the creation process. Reading it through and editing as you experience new revelations about what's important to you is the creative power behind your story and the pathway to getting exactly what is most important to you. When you read your completed story in its final form, you will likely feel a physical shift, accompanied by tingling sensations inside. You'll experience a sense of hope, optimism, even exhilaration; but more important, you'll have empowering knowledge, clarity, and a stronger sense of your true self. Now you're ready to move onto attracting your Dream Man into your life.

BETWEEN YOU AND ME:
Guess Who's Coming to Dinner

My Dream Man had three small boys when I met him. He was fifty and I was forty-seven, with a twenty-three-year-old daughter. There was nothing in my story about having small children in my life, and I never imagined I would become a stepmother in my late forties. However, I found that raising his children was the best thing that could have happened to my life. I had a second chance to create a bustling home life that was very different from the one I'd experienced with my daughter who was an only child. I hadn't realized this was something I deeply desired. As a result, the Dream Man Story Creator now includes more categories and questions designed to provide you with clarity on all the Big Questions. It's still my Dream Man's strongest qualities, essence, and values that make our marriage work today; it's not the specific events and circumstances that have occurred in our lives. Remember, you're looking for a man who complements and satisfies your deepest desires, and he may come packaged in a way that you never expected. Keep an open mind.

Now what?

Reflect

Create

Attract

STEP 3. *Attract—Manifest Your Own Ending*

"Your energy speaks louder than words; be aware of what signals you're sending."

Congratulations on completing the Story Creator. You are now clear about what you want. Now that you've filled in the blanks, you have a deeper sense of what you're looking for in your Dream Man through magnetic resonance. But the process isn't quite finished yet. This final section guides you through the process of attracting your Dream Man. Be sure to type or write out your story in full. Reading the story in its final form is a critical part of embodying it and igniting the attraction factor. You've done all this hard work—don't stop now or the process won't be complete.

ENERGETIC COMPATIBILITY AND MAGNETIC RESONANCE

While you're reading your Dream Man story, you should have a smile on your face, a sense of fulfillment, and a powerful connection to your man. It can be exhilarating. You will actually *see* and *feel* your life with the man of your dreams.

When you bring your Dream Man story to life, you will begin to attract men with complementary energy who resonate with your deepest desires. This will support you to find someone who's energetically compatible, which is what he'll be looking for, too. Compatibility is based on mutually harmonious and congenial feelings. By internalizing your clear vision with feelings and declaring your truest desires, you will change your resonance and attraction factor. You'll see men differently and they'll see you differently, too. Most women try to make their dreams come true by directing their thoughts out into the world with lists, wishful thinking, and hope. However, attraction actually happens through changing your energetic resonance to bring your dreams to you. Your Dream Man story creates and empowers this magnetic resonance.

ENERGY SPEAKS LOUDER THAN WORDS

You've probably met people with intense energy who either repelled or attracted you. Your body is a system comprised of energy centers that receive and emit electromagnetic force fields. (If you want more information on this, I recommend *The Heart of the Soul* by Gary Zukav.) Your deep beliefs and thoughts create feelings and emotions that radiate either positive or negative force fields—your energy. This occurs constantly, whether you like it or not, and your energy can be subtly seen and felt by others. While others may not always accurately or consciously identify your feelings, they can sense either a positive or negative vibration. Your feelings are sending out energetic signals that resonate and attract matching energy—and you can't fake it. Your energy speaks louder than your words. For example, if you carry around a deep-seated belief that ultimately all men are destined to cheat, you are more likely to attract men who will fulfill your belief. Doesn't it make sense, then, to change your thought patterns and beliefs to what you *want* rather than what you don't want? What you do is minuscule compared with what you choose to think. Thoughts are powerful, and they are the only thing in our lives that we can actually control. But you can't create what you want from your mind alone. You need the emotional connection of your thoughts with your feelings. Our bodies respond to our emotions, either positively or negatively. You know you're connecting with your feelings when you can feel energy and emotional reactions in your body.

THOUGHTS + FEELINGS = CREATION

There are numerous books and films on the Law of Attraction, and the principle has been embraced by some of the greatest achievers of the twentieth century. In his 1937 book, *Think and Grow Rich*, Napoleon Hill wrote, "Any idea, plan or purpose that is brought into the conscious mind and repeatedly supported by emotional feeling is automatically picked up by the subconscious brain and carried out to its conclusion." He extolled the power of visualization and burning desire (feelings) as the secret to having anything you want. Other contemporary self-help authors and speakers—Gary Zukav, Dr. Wayne Dyer, and Dr. Deepak Chopra, to name a few—speak passionately about the power of intention in creating your life through focused thoughts and attention on what you desire. More recently, the phenomenon of *The Secret* has swept the world. It is an inspirational introduction and illustration of the power of attraction.

I like the Wikipedia definition of the Law of Attraction:

"People's thoughts (both conscious and unconscious) dictate the reality of their lives, whether or not they're aware of it. If you really want something and truly believe it's possible, you'll get it. The Law of Attraction claims to have roots in Quantum Physics. According to proponents of this law, thoughts have an energy which attracts whatever it is the person is thinking of. In order to control this energy to one's advantage, proponents state that people must practice four things:

1. Know exactly what you want.
2. Ask the universe for it.
3. Feel, behave, and know as if the object of your desire is on its way.
4. Be open to receive it and let go of the attachment to the outcome.

Thinking of what one does not have, they say, manifests itself in not having, while if one abides by these principles and avoids negative thoughts, the universe will manifest a person's desires."

For more information on how this powerful law relates to relationships, I recommend Esther and Jerry Hicks' *The Vortex: Where the Law of Attraction Assembles All Cooperative Relationships.*

NOW WHAT DO I DO WITH MY DREAM MAN STORY?

1. **KEEP FINE-TUNING** until it feels complete to you. Condense it to reflect only what's important to you.

2. **READ YOUR DREAM MAN STORY EVERY DAY** for a couple of weeks or more. Reading it aloud while envisioning it in your mind can add even more juice to the process and make it feel more real. Your goal is to create new neural pathways in your brain for your new beliefs and attitudes. You want them deeply embedded in your subconscious so that your magnetic resonance sends a clear signal. This time frame for reviewing your story varies among women; it's based on when you feel a sense of completeness. It needs to become part of your cellular fabric. I read mine every night for two weeks before I went to sleep, which helped me to fully embrace and embody my story. The first week I found myself tweaking it to be more specific and adding things I'd missed. You'll know when you embody your vision because it will feel good in your heart and you can speak to others about what you want clearly and decisively. The purpose of the process and story is to extract your truest dream, see it in writing, feel it, claim it, and fully embody it. You are clear-headed and heart-connected and have spent a lot of time thinking and writing about what you truly want, so you can't pretend it doesn't exist or devalue anything you've written. Your goal is to see your life with this man all the way into feeling the emotions of having him in your life. When you read your story, feel the feelings of every aspect of what you've envisioned. This is the secret to transforming your energy to create magnetic resonance, which will draw him to you like a hummingbird to nectar.

3. **KEEP YOUR STORY HANDY.** Keep it within easy access—in your desk, journal, or nightstand—to review whenever you need a reminder. There's no need to be overly preoccupied or intensely focused on your story beyond the first several weeks. You now emanate the energy and resonance of your vision, and your actions move you towards your goal.

4. **EDIT AND UPDATE** it as you date. As you change and grow, make sure your story matches your growth. Updating your story will reap great results in renewing the energy you radiate.

5. PRACTICE. View each new man you date as practice in moving a step closer to your ideal man. Keep notes on the men who are not a match to see if they have similarities with each other (revisit the "Themes That Didn't Work for Me" activity under "What I Don't Want" in Part 1). If they do, this may be a clue that something inside you still is resisting the man of your dreams. Ask yourself what inside you is causing attraction to the same traits or patterns in men. When you remain aware and start to notice patterns, it is far easier to redefine what you "deserve" and focus your attention on releasing the block in your energy and magnetic resonance.

6. SHARE IT WITH A POTENTIAL DREAM MAN. When you think you've found a man who may be the one, if you're comfortable, show him your Dream Man story and see what he thinks. WARNING: Be certain that you share a mutual intention towards each other first. Revealing this too soon could be overwhelming to him. When I eventually showed my husband my story, he took everything to heart, remembers what it said to this day, and does his best to remain my Dream Man.

7. USE IT TO WRITE YOUR AUTHENTIC BIO. Use all of this insight to create your online dating bio that proclaims the authentic you and what you're looking for in a man. That is tantamount to sending your electromagnetic signal over the Internet. Focus on what you want rather than what you think he's looking for.

8. LIVE YOUR IDEAL RELATIONSHIPS WITH EVERYONE IN YOUR LIFE. Look at what you've discovered about your patterns, values, and desires. You'll likely find yourself interacting in a more empowered way with other people and situations in your life, both personally and professionally.

Radiate Your New Energy

You are now ready to employ your attraction techniques. You've cleared out your old beliefs; identified who you are and what you love and value; and created your Dream Man story and hand-written or typed it in full. Now you're ready to ignite the attraction factor that draws him right into your life. While the preliminary activities and creation of your story began the process of transformation, reading the vision helps you fully integrate your new way of being. Your energy is shifting to be more in alignment with the new beliefs, thoughts, and feelings evoked from reading your story. Once you cement these new thoughts and feelings in your body, you've claimed them and you aren't going to lose them. You naturally begin to radiate a new energy of self-knowledge and a clear vision of your man and your relationship. This causes you to resonate a powerful magnetic signal that broadcasts: This is who I am, this is the man I want, and this is the relationship I deserve to have.

PART 5. *What To Expect Next*

"Radiate your feminine potential, attract the man of your dreams, and you will change the world."

MY PERFECTLY IMPERFECT DREAM MAN

You may be wondering: *Is my Dream Man going to have every quality I describe in my story?* He might, but more likely he'll possess most, but not all, of those qualities. Then again, you may also get more than you imagined. You can expect to attract a man who embodies your most deeply cherished qualities. Your priorities will also become clear without your having to think about them. You'll notice more men coming into your life with more of the qualities you want, but you'll no longer waste time on men who aren't an energetic and complementary match. You'll sense and assess men through the filter of your core values rather than through your old programming, outdated fantasies, and misleading surface evaluations.

Are you saying he's going to be a perfect man who does everything right, and that we'll never have problems? Absolutely not. Being human is about making mistakes, facing challenges, and

overcoming obstacles—mixed in with pleasurable experiences, personal fulfillment, and joy. The man of your dreams is someone who fulfills your deepest desires and complements your way of navigating the highs and lows of life. After the sizzle fades, you want to know you're with a man who nourishes your heart and soul through any adversity.

How long will it take to find my Dream Man? This isn't possible for me to answer since it depends so much on two people's personal circumstances and divine timing. However, your part in the equation is to make sure you are breaking through old patterns and healing the places inside you that resist having him in your life. See the Related Reading in Appendix A if you're interested in additional resources to assist you in healing emotional blocks and patterns. I met my husband eleven months after I wrote my story, but other women have met theirs sooner and others have taken longer.

EXPECT SURPRISES

Paradoxically, while your actual Dream Man might not look exactly like the mental picture you've conjured, you'll begin to recognize energetic synchronicity from your Dream Man story. You're attracting his energy and the feelings you want to experience and not exclusively the external package. He might show up with qualities and new experiences you hadn't expected, and those can add new and wonderful dimensions to your life that you hadn't anticipated. Just as your home's interior design can be changed and enhanced dramatically by a fabulous piece of furniture you find, so too can your relationship be improved by a Dream Man who brings delightful and unexpected attributes.

Through this process, the more you learn about what you love and what's important to you, the more options for men open up to you. This process encourages you to create new relationship visions that are less superficial. Keep an open mind to allow a relationship to flow naturally.

ARIELLE'S STORY:
An Unexpected Dream Man Package

After swearing off of online dating for six months, Arielle decided to sign up with a new matchmaking site, only this time it was going to be different. Dating was so stressful because she was always doubting her own acceptability and was looking for validation from the men she met. "I was so tired of feeling badly about myself from two failed marriages, childhood baggage, and thinking I was defective, and I was tired of waiting for a man to start my life," she said. She made a pact with herself to get happy in her life and start to be grateful and truly receive and value what she already had, especially all of her good friends.

She decided that this time, instead of a very general profile listing the qualities she wanted in a man, she was going to be very specific and ask for exactly what she wanted. In the past she was hesitant to be too specific for fear she would discourage too many prospects and didn't want to seem like a "picky bitch." This time she had an attitude that she would post only one photo instead of the usual seven, and focus her profile on what she was looking for rather than describing so much about herself. When Arielle was contacted by Sol, she looked at the photo and saw that he was overweight and not her type at all. Even a couple of comments he had in his profile disturbed her, but she couldn't tell if he was serious or trying to be funny. He continued to pursue her, so she finally decided to meet him for coffee, hoping he would look more attractive in person. Well, he didn't, and she was disappointed. But he was so entertaining and interesting and they had so much in common that by the end of their two-hour coffee date, Arielle noticed that Sol had become more attractive. She continued to see him, and with each subsequent date Sol became increasingly more attractive. His wonderful personality, kindness, and genuine nature transformed his looks. It's been eight months since they met, and things are going strong. Arielle said, "He matches 99 percent of everything I wanted in my Dream Man. He's sensitive, romantic, thoughtful, hardworking, and has a big life. There's nothing nagging at me thinking there could be someone better for me."

WHAT TO KNOW BEFORE DIVING INTO DATING

It's important to understand that your new beliefs don't change the realities of your hormones and biological makeup. Here are some things that can get you into trouble:

Dance of the Magical Hormones

During the early stage of dating, it's common for men and women to present themselves in the most positive light. The instinctual primitive mating dance begins, in which a couple exhibits newfound energy, performs at their peak, and struts their best attributes. They're compelled to impress each other, and therefore become more interesting, exciting, romantic, and uplifting. A strong physical attraction stimulates the release of chemicals commonly called love hormones, including adrenalin, dopamine, and endorphins, that trigger a state of euphoria in couples. This rapturous elation seems to cause each of their lives to suddenly make sense; it's exhilarating, sparking optimism about unlimited potential for their life together. Passion connects their hearts to beat as one, emanating a palpable sense of completeness. *This could be it—The One.* They naturally fall into playing roles for each other's unspoken illusion that this person is certain to make the other's life fulfilling, secure, meaningful, and joyful—forever. *I'll play the part you want and you'll play the part I want.* Their hormonal high emboldens them to delude each other with fantasies about who they *think* they are, who they *wish they were,* or perhaps who they *used to be in high school*. Unfortunately, it's often not who they *actually* are now—nor is it likely this is who they will ever be. This is a temporary, fleeting state.

Chemical Bondage

This is the magical dance of coupling that we crave and are addicted to like an illicit drug. Similar to a drug high, our judgment is severely impaired during this ecstatic and blissful state. We're seduced by the hormonal hallucinogens whirling in our heads and titillating our loins. Over time, however, as the hormones gradually stabilize and we return to our natural state, we suddenly begin to notice the conspicuous flaws in our formerly perfect mate—and we no longer desire to play our part anymore.

During intense emotional states, and particularly with orgasm, women and men release a hormone (oxytocin) that stimulates bonding and attachment to their partner. Testosterone somewhat neutralizes oxytocin in men, and women produce substantially more of the chemical, which means women form stronger attachments. Our primitive nesting instinct kicks into gear, and we become trapped in emotional addiction, blinded to a man's blatant defects. But it's too late: We're hooked. Our lover becomes our drug dealer and we become junkies willing to sacrifice our needs, dreams, friends, and even our self-respect for our next fix.

What woman hasn't overdosed from the out-of-control spiral into chemical bondage? I know I've been there, done that. Symptoms show up in many forms. How many do you remember displaying? Go ahead and circle all that apply:

- Falling in love with a man's potential instead of seeing who he really is right now.
- Putting your life on hold and his priorities ahead of yours.
- Feeling rejected and devastated when he doesn't call.
- Competing with other women when you're not even sure he's right for you.
- Snooping through his email account and text messages and rifling through his pockets and drawers for clues.
- Doing drive-bys or surveillance on his house to check if he's home.
- Sending yourself flowers "from an old boyfriend" to make him jealous.
- Disliking or being jealous of his old girlfriend for no particular reason.
- Trying to convince yourself and everyone else you know that he is The One.

If you've ever indulged in that sort of behavior, what have you learned from it now that you've changed your old patterns and beliefs about the type of relationship you want to be in? What are some warning signs that might tempt you to revert to this type of behavior?

_____
_____
_____

_____
_____
_____
_____
_____
_____.

Plead Temporary Insanity

Please know it is possible to neutralize our hormonally induced, temporary insanity. The first step is to be aware of what's causing this wacky, desperate behavior. My point is that since we know these behaviors are symptomatic of the traditional (and outdated) mating game, it's crucial to be prepared with an antidote to jolt us back into reality and remind us what truly matters for the long term. Your Dream Man story is your antidote. Think of it as your internal speedometer that enables you to gauge how fast you're going before you speed out of control from lust and chemical bondage. Your story is your reality check, a tangible reference tool, similar to a roadmap that leads to your destiny. It guides you back to your path and helps you avoid getting sidetracked by transient hitchhikers.

SHELLY'S STORY:
Chemical Bondage and Unrequited Love Turning into Desperation

Shelly's story is a classic. She was at her wit's end, wondering if she was far more in love with her man than he was with her. She was certain he was The One, but he wasn't matching her intensity, and it was driving her bonkers. "One day I knew I had to have an answer or I was going to rip my hair out," she confided. "So I waited outside his office for him to leave work. Then I emerged from behind some bushes wearing a big sign around my neck with large red letters. It said: LOVE ME OR SHOOT ME. I wasn't kidding. Michael must have read the desperation in my eyes, because he came towards me as if approaching a feral cat. But then he took my hand and broke off our relationship right there in the parking lot. In some ways it was a relief. At least I had my answer. I just wish I knew then what I know now."

DEALING WITH THE PARADOX

Now for what can be the most difficult part—detaching from the outcome. You may be thinking, *How can I feel the feelings of having him and then let go of attachment to outcome?* What this means is that while you've identified and embraced the feelings of what you want, you don't try to force or manipulate the outcome. Releasing inner resistance and letting go of attachment to outcome is trusting the process and *allowing* it to happen naturally. Allowing comes from a place of trust and creates an opening and space for what you want. When you try to force or manipulate a relationship, it comes from a place of fear and control and is constricting and repelling, which sends out energetic signals of desperation and doubt. Remember, choosing is not chasing. Allowing is surrendering to trust and a sense of deserving what's right for you. Letting go of outcome is trusting that there are many available choices, an abundant farmers' market. It's the ultimate honoring of yourself. Every time your thoughts wander to fear or self-doubt, you must pull them back to what you deserve, then center yourself in trust and patience.

BETWEEN YOU AND ME: *What's Right For Me*

Even after I met my Dream Man, I had to remain in surrender and allowing. He was seeing a twenty-five-year-old woman (half his age) and was dating both of us simultaneously. While I was attracted to him, I remained in observation mode and released my attachment to the outcome. Did I have a momentary shake when I knew he was out with her? Yes, because I'm human, but it quickly passed when I would remind myself that I could only be content with a man who wanted me as much as I wanted him. I wasn't jealous and felt no need to compete with a woman who was twenty years younger. I didn't need to pass judgment on him for dating a younger woman. I was still observing him in different situations to see how well he matched my needs. Why would I compete to win him over? It was not a contest; it was my life and I was choosing. I would mentally refer back to my story and say to myself, If she's who he wants, then he's not right for me. I never brought her name up to him or questioned his whereabouts.

After about two months, he ended up telling the younger woman that he was in love with me. She asked him to go with her to a one-time counseling session to help her get through their break-up. He asked me if it was okay with me to do this. I told him I understood how she must feel and that it was a good idea. They went to the session and their relationship ended. Did I do a victory dance? No, I felt empathy for her. I'd been there myself, and I observed a new facet of my Dream Man's sensitivity and integrity.

REMAIN IN OBSERVATION MODE AND AVOID DESPERATION

In my journey to attract my Dream Man, I continually reminded myself that I was choosing the man of my dreams—not waiting to be chosen by him or changing who I was to fit into his world. When I dated, I would mentally refer to my Dream Man story and notice whether my date's qualities matched my needs. I also paid attention to my feelings. Did his way of being and behavior resonate with my heart's desires? I call this practice *observation mode*. There's a distinct difference between *observation mode* and *desperation mode*, which is described below. I also noticed that when I did meet my Dream Man, everything flowed naturally. Nothing was forced, and there was no need to fix anything about who he was inside (his essence) or how he treated me. To this day, he's the same wonderful man I was first attracted to, and he treats me with the same respect and love that he did when I met him.

One of these modes will get you what you want and the other will leave you miserable (or, at a minimum, stuck in short-lived romances). You're going to begin to attract men with a lot of the qualities in your story. Refrain from "fishing from the shallows" by immediately jumping to the conclusion that *this must be him*. Take your time and remain in *observation mode* for at least a few months, even if he seems absolutely perfect. Make sure he fits your desires and needs and that he really is who you believe him to be. As I mentioned, we're usually on our best behavior during the first two or three months of a relationship, so give it some time. You can have fun, play in the hormonal high, feel as if you're falling in love—but frequently take breathers and check in with what you've observed about this man. What is real and lasting and what is temporary fantasy? One of my recent clients told me that she isn't latching onto any particular one of the new, wonderful men who've begun to appear—she's keeping her options open and excited about who will show up next. She knows she has choices.

OBSERVATION MODE DEFINED

This is the time to be ever-watchful of a man's behavior and patterns to see whether there is energetic compatibility or not. Contemplate the following questions:

- What questions does he ask about you? Is he interested in your work, background, friends, hobbies, things you like to do, etc?
- How well does he listen to you and to others?
- Does he allow room or give you a sense of freedom to be more of who you are?
- Is he supportive and encouraging about your aspirations? Is he even curious?
- How does he treat you and other people in different situations?
- What red flags appear? The matching qualities will be obvious, but pay attention to the qualities that don't match. What are his subtle mismatching qualities that contradict the essence of your Dream Man story?
- See how you feel with him around different groups of people, such as his family, coworkers, and friends; during activities or sports and in public; notice how he treats service people in restaurants, retail stores, or maintenance people.
- How is he in traffic or a stressful situation?
- How does he speak about his previous relationships and women he has dated?
- What are his communication habits and opinions about the world, how considerate is he of you and others?
- What's his work ethic and what are his feelings about his career and future goals?
- How jealous, possessive, or secure is he?

- How generous is he with you and his friends?
- How honest is he, and does he have integrity?
- How does he handle conflict or disagreements with you and others?

Observation mode is about staying realistic and seeing him as he really is and not thinking you can make him into someone you think he can be (his potential is *your* fantasy). Observation mode means noticing how you feel in each situation and asking yourself important questions:

- Can you live with this forever, 24/7?
- Is this what you truly want?
- Does this behavior give you energy or drain your energy?
- Would you want your sister, daughter, or friend involved in this kind of relationship? Is it what you would dream for them? Would it be empowering or disempowering; would they flourish or shrink?
- Do you feel safe, natural, and at ease with him? Or do you feel anxious, uncomfortable, or like you're trying too hard to please or impress him?
- Based on your Dream Man story, what other questions should you ask yourself to see if this is a true dream match?

_____
_____
_____
_____
_____
_____
_____
_____
_____.

Keep in mind that observation is not the same as judgment, which implies you're looking for things that are wrong with him. Observation is focusing your attention on what is right for you. It's a totally different mindset and way of being that is very empowering to you and is not negative or condescending to anyone.

In observation mode, you can lie in bed at night and feel happy and grateful for the life you're creating and trust that the right man will show up soon. You can take pride in your internal knowing that you deserve a wonderful relationship with the man of your dreams. You can let go of the outcome and know in your heart that you'll attain what you want in a man or be happy and at peace remaining single. Observation mode is living in your newly empowered belief system. Observation mode feels peaceful, trusting, and patient.

GEORGIA'S STORY:
Learning The Difference Between Intuitive Feelings And Emotional Fantasy

Georgia is a thirty-eight-year-old client who had been divorced for two years when she completed the Choose Him Process. Within two weeks, she met the man she believed was "him" and called to tell me what a perfect match he was to everything she wanted. She became so emotional about meeting this perfect man immediately after creating him that she actually burst into tears within the first fifteen minutes of their first meeting. He treated her wonderfully and did not make her feel foolish in any way. She dated him a few times and everything seemed to be going so well, until he suggested that they continue to date other people since he had only recently left a twenty-five-year marriage. Georgia was reeling from this suggestion since she felt they were a perfect match. She began to pursue him, believing that she was "choosing" him and going after what she wanted. Even though she professed to understand observation mode and the concept of not forcing romance, she insisted that she had dated many, many men and this man was perfect and absolutely had to be The One. Two weeks later, he called to let her know that he had met someone else.

She now understands why you must take your time and remain in observation and not get carried away with your emotions and fantasy-come-true patterns that slip you into desperation mode. Remember, there is more than one man out there for you who is an ideal match.

DESPERATION MODE DEFINED

In this mode, you so desperately want a partner that you try hard to see only the best in the men you meet and ignore the red flags.

- You see bad behavior or patterns that conflict with your standards and you still ignore them or pretend they aren't important.
- You believe that if only he'd just change this or that, he'd be perfect.
- You are so turned on by him that you think the sex could overcome anything and make the relationship last forever.
- You think that if he would just not fear intimacy that he'd realize how important you are to him; if he would only give your love a chance, he'd be so happy.
- You psychoanalyze and believe you have the ultimate answers to all he needs, and you're sure he can find happiness with you, even though he's done nothing to consistently invest in the relationship.

Desperation mode is feeling that there are so few available men out there that you need to compromise and work hard to hang onto a negative relationship for fear of being alone. Desperation is having so little self-esteem and love for yourself that you have to convince a man to love you. It's about believing that what he thinks of you—and whether he loves you or not—is more important than what you think of yourself. It's when you're waiting for a man to come into your life before you begin to live and love your own life. It's believing the fantasy that you will begin to value and love yourself *after* the man shows up. Living in desperation mode is your own special pity party lying in bed at night and asking yourself: Is this all there is to life? Why can't I find someone to share my life who truly loves me? What's wrong with me? You find yourself asking yourself and your girlfriends: Do you think he loves me? Do you think he's just scared? Why doesn't he call? Is he seeing someone else? Will he quit drinking/flirting/cheating . . . for me? You can tell by the feeling in your body if your questions are coming from observation or desperation. Desperation mode feels like anxiety, self-doubt, and fear.

Desperation mode is your old belief system and old thought patterns in action. It tells you why you need to settle, what you can't have, what won't ever be, and why it will never work for you. A multitude of books and movies show cultural examples of desperation mode in action. Often the women who do win the guy have to play games and pretend to be confident and someone they're not. This type of deception does not lead  to a lasting romance in real life. You now have a tool that gives you a genuine basis for observation—your Dream Man story. You don't have to pretend you're a woman with high standards who knows her worth and what she wants. You really are.

CASSIE'S STORY: *Patience Is a Pleasure*

"Having recently done the Choose Him Process, there have been some distinct and unanticipated results. I have noticed that I am meeting more men. In fact, I have met more interesting men in the past two months than I have in the past two years. The other thing I'm noticing is that more men take the time to notice me. I get more looks. I'm also discovering authentic flirtation. By this I mean telling the truth in a fun way without using it as a means to an end. I can tell a man that he has a gorgeous smile without trying to entice him into asking me out.

I hadn't anticipated how much more fun things could get. I'm more interested in enjoying the process and meeting more beautiful men than my old determination to seek, find, and close the deal. These are all welcome surprises. I'm physically experiencing this new compelling feeling and finding myself strolling through my life in a way that's entirely different from the way I used to rush around. I'm having more fun than ever and finding that patience is no longer a virtue, but a pleasure."

YOUR TOP 5 TO 10 RESONANCE LIST

After all this intense self-examination, there's one more list that could serve you well: your Top 5 to 10 Resonance List. Below list the internal qualities that you simply must have in a partner—things that must resonate with your heart and your core. They might include: respectful, trustworthy, patient, responsible, open-minded, curious, generous, good-hearted, kind, sense of humor, good listener, etc. These are not the usual external or negative qualities that we typically think of as deal breakers (i.e. non-smoker, having a job, etc.). Go back to your story and highlight the words or phrases that light you up, touch your heart, and feel good.

_____
_____
_____
_____
_____
_____
_____
_____
_____
_____
_____
_____
_____
_____.

DEB'S 15 PERSONAL POWER BOOSTS AND POWER LEAKS

Here are some additional tips that may help you navigate the dating world. Power boosts are things you think, do, and talk about to keep you focused on what you want and in charge of your energy. Personal power leaks are patterns we slip into that don't serve us or the guy. They consist of any actions or old ways of doing things that are not genuine or that tend to backfire on us in romance. These situations typically end up with you feeling let down, empty inside, and doubting yourself. Your confidence is shaken, confusion sets in, and your magnetic energy starts to drain away.

1. BELIEVE YOUR DREAM MAN WILL APPEAR. Get in touch with the part of you that knows you're worth having him. Review your lists of what you love and value about yourself.

2. START BEING WHO YOU ARE WITH HIM NOW. Live your life to its fullest and do what makes you feel good and have fun NOW—don't wait for the man first. His job is not to make you happy. He wants to meet a fulfilled woman who is already happy and who brings her authenticity and joy to the relationship. You want to attract a man who's an energetic echo and match to you, so start being what you want to attract.

3. LOOK BEYOND WHAT YOU SEE. Don't be too quick to judge men by their appearance. Your Dream Man may not come in the package you have in your mind. Remember, the right guy may be disguised in weird hair and outdated or unstylish clothes. You can't change him inside, but sometimes you need to polish him up on the outside. A man wants to please a woman who sees the worthy attributes that he brings to the relationship. Men who feel appreciated will go to great lengths to earn more of that precious appreciation, so keep it coming. Also, I know plenty of women who have had zero chemistry with a man until after they get to know him better. These men turned out to be so wonderful that the women became sexually turned on by them because of the way the men treated them, their humor, personality, values, and ways of being.

4. **REFER TO YOUR STORY AND ASK QUESTIONS.** When you're on a date, take time to ask questions and explore whether this man matches your Dream Man story. *You get to choose. You get to choose. You get to choose.* I'm not talking about going down your checklist as if in an interview, but rather general topics about what he likes to do, his feelings on travel or where he's been, friends, special interests, work, movies, etc. Do you feel a need to chatter uncomfortably or promote yourself instead of being natural and curious about him and allowing the conversation to flow? Really listen to what he says. There are rich conversation starters within your Dream Man story—use them.

5. **DON'T BE A CHAMELEON.** Watch your thoughts and behavior as you meet men. What thinking patterns, judgments, and beliefs do you experience? Do you change your behavior and become a chameleon with each new man, hoping that he'll like that personality? You now are clear about who you are and what you care about, so be authentic and honest and don't worry about whether he's going to judge you or reject you. If he does, then he's not right for you.

6. **YOU'RE NOT HIS MAMA!** Please don't make the mistake of thinking you'll become his inspiration to finally do the things he talks about. And definitely don't believe you'll be the special woman who changes him. How many women do you know who have succeeded in creating a Dream Man out of an unwilling or pitiful candidate? Again, this is an old fantasy we've seen repeatedly in fairytales and movies: the spunky little woman who comes along and turns his life around—rescues the bad boy, unhappily married man, playboy, depressed artist, alcoholic musician—you name it. The fantasy is that he's so grateful and inspired by her for saving him and making him change his ways that he promises to love and admire her forever. Uh, no. Can we please stop thinking this is the way we're supposed to get a man? When the right guy comes along, it should be comfortable and easy—free from drama and problems that you need to fix before the relationship can work.

7. **PLEASE, PLEASE, PLEASE DON'T.** Are you one of those women who likes to please everyone, especially men? Is your focus outward toward others rather than inward on what you feel and need? Do you relinquish your self-worth into the hands of a man and then shrink or feel hurt when you're not appreciated? You can still be a kind and considerate person without constantly focusing on what you think a man wants and needs. It isn't necessary to prove how flexible, understanding, and easy-to-be-with you are. That behavior doesn't endear you or make you more valued by a man. And worse, in the process you renounce your personal power and self-esteem and you don't reveal your true personality and

authenticity to him. You will likely cause him to feel disconnected, bored, or wonder who you really are and what you have to offer in a relationship. Or worse yet, he may start to take advantage of you (I don't use the "doormat" word lightly), which will chip away at your personal power.

8. GET OUT OF HIS HEAD. Okay, here's another big one that diminishes our personal power. It's an obsessive need to psychoanalyze and come up with solutions to fix a man's issues. When he fails to be exactly what we want (or even if he is), we may start to analyze everything—his possible childhood problems, work predicament, ex-wife/girlfriend/children troubles, and even what he must be thinking. We love to go over every word he said to us with our girlfriends, get their opinions, and then become the self-appointed therapists who know just what he needs to solve his problem. It takes a lot of energy to play in a guy's head, and it gets you nowhere. The easier alternative is to just allow the relationship to unfold naturally and do everything possible to avoid figuring out what he's thinking. Stay on the track of what you want long-term.

9. GET OUT OF HIS POCKET. We can also be looking in his pocket, so to speak. If we think or know that a guy is having financial troubles, we often begin to compromise what we want. This initiates the trickle-down effect of compromise in other areas of the relationship. We start deciding what he can or can't afford, how we can help him with his problems, what we no longer need since we don't want to appear too money-focused, and so on. *(Oh, that's okay, I don't need popcorn at the movies; I've always wanted to have a vacation adventure on a Greyhound bus; here, let me buy this for you.)* You get the picture. Stay out of his pocket. Let him tell you what he wants to do and what he can or cannot afford. Then you decide if you want to go along with his idea or offer to pay. If you aren't open and genuine, he will know you're trying to protect his ego, and that's equivalent to emasculating him—the opposite of what you're trying to do. We can spend so much wasted energy scrutinizing his life and how we might fit into it that we lose ourselves and compromise what we want. We leak our personal power by the slow-drip method, and it seeps away until we find ourselves feeling diminished, disillusioned, and desperate.

10. AGAIN, WATCH THOSE HORMONES. Oh boy, this is like catnip to a kitten. I've talked about the love hormones that rush through your body and lure you into a drugged state of lust and romance. You feel like you're falling head over heels in love and that there's nothing more exciting and important than to be with him. It feels like this can only happen with someone you're meant to be with forever. Remember, love-struck hormones chemically alter you and can dupe you into doing and believing things that are not real.

Keep in mind that the feeling is temporary and can delude you into false euphoria about the long-term potential of a relationship. Sex is not a permanent glue. Keep observing.

11. JUST SAY NO. If he's not right for you, let him know as soon as possible. Often, we're so afraid of the void that we cling to sub-standard men and relationships. Releasing a man who's not a good match allows space in your life for someone who is. Women have such a hard time with this one. We've been taught to be very careful with a man's ego and to not hurt his feelings. Women are naturally empathetic (we feel your pain), and we tend not to want to say something that we wouldn't want said to us. Would you prefer he just not call you, hide from you, or make up a story about going back with an old girlfriend? Practice learning how to say it doesn't work—simply and directly. Just the facts without fabricated stories or whiny apologies. A polite "I'm sorry" will do. The more you practice, the easier it gets and the more empowered you'll feel. It's not your duty to preserve a man's ego by tiptoeing around the truth.

Here are some simple, direct, polite examples:

You're a great guy, so I'm sorry it doesn't feel like we're a fit.

It's been nice meeting you, but I don't feel we're a match.

This has been an enjoyable meeting, but it's just not right for me.

I've had a lot of fun with you, but I'm sorry that we don't have enough things (beliefs, values, lifestyle habits) in common.

I care about you a lot, but I see us more as friends than as a couple (partners). I would love to do things with you but I don't see this moving in the direction of a romantic relationship.

I really wish this could have worked out, but I'm sorry it just doesn't feel right for me.

While there are many things that we have in common, after deep consideration I feel strongly that there is not a further match between us.

Thank you for the adventures and life we shared. I wish you the absolute best on your journey. You're a wonderful man.

12. **DON'T TAKE REJECTION PERSONALLY.** Keep in mind that if there isn't an energetic match or sexual chemistry, THAT IS NOT A REJECTION of him. Your physical attraction to each other is beyond your control. It really is chemical, and you can't force either of you to feel something that isn't there. This has nothing to do with the looks or value of a person. This goes for you, too, so don't think there's something wrong with you simply because a man says you're not right for each other. Let's face it—you aren't going to fit every man's ideal of beauty, sexiness, or personality. Why should you take that as a rejection? No matter how gorgeous or hot he is, don't make any man the global authority on your appeal.

    After the initial connection (which may be based on physical appearance), lasting attraction is based mostly on energy and how you feel about each other. We've all seen numerous examples of stereotypically handsome men with very plain, unsexy, or overweight women, as well as the reverse scenario with pretty women. Isn't that one of the fears that many women express—that we aren't pretty, sexy, or thin enough according to the social standards we've bought into? We've all heard men criticize the looks and sex appeal of female celebrities who we consider the most beautiful and desirable. Then we freak out and worry about our own attractiveness. I believe there IS a Dream Man for every woman, and he will think she's beautiful regardless of her shape, size, brains, or personality. Different qualities and energy appeal to different people, and none of us will ever be universally perfect for every man.

13. **WATCH YOUR ENERGY.** Whenever you start to fall for a man, keep reminding yourself that you're in *observation mode* and don't allow your emotions to sweep you into a state of romantic fantasy: *this must be it* and *he's The One*. He will feel the pressure in your energy—don't be surprised if he disappears. Remember, your thoughts and beliefs automatically create your energy. Give yourself time to truly know he's right for you. It's not a game. Also, you won't discourage him by not being swept away by his romantic overtures or strong desire to be with you. If a man is interested in you, he will pursue you.

14. **HONOR YOUR FEELINGS.** Now that you're clear about what you want, it will become more difficult to dismiss or discount your feelings. Let your intuitive feelings be your guide to know if you're in observation or desperation mode. Since you now have standards for what you want, you'll notice you're reacting in a more empowered way. If something doesn't feel good, don't try to justify why you're putting up with it. You will be proud of yourself when you state your requirements calmly, clearly, and confidently. True personal power has nothing to do with being demanding, convincing, or forceful with your energy. It

doesn't employ emotional tactics, overbearing behavior, or manipulation. When you make a conscious decision or choice from a place of present-moment awareness and clarity—knowing what you feel, what you want, what is real, and what is really happening—you will experience authentic personal power. For more information on this topic, see Related Reading at the end of the book.

15. R̲e̲r̲e̲a̲d̲ ̲y̲o̲u̲r̲ ̲s̲t̲o̲r̲y̲. It's not uncommon to make some of your old mistakes as you integrate this new information and way of being. Whenever you feel you've veered off track or are repeating old beliefs and patterns, reread your story and review your new beliefs. It's fun to read it and look for resonance when you meet a man who seems to fit your story. But please don't try to *make* him your Dream Man and compromise or ignore red flags just because he has many of the qualities in your story.

THE NEW TRUE YOU—CONGRATULATIONS!

You are different now. You have transformed yourself and your ideas, and you should feel something has shifted inside you. You've changed your perspective and have newly tuned judgment and perception. When checking your values and desires against the men who show up, you can trust your newly found core voice to tell you what is and is not a dream match for you. You've reprogrammed old limiting beliefs, articulated your authentic values and desires, and declared you're a woman who knows her worth. You know more about the language of attraction by moving your thoughts and conversation away from negative patterns of what you don't want into the positive expression of what you do want.

You've created a picture of the man of your dreams through a clear lens and open heart and embraced the feelings inherent in your creation. Now you can review and refine your story until it feels just right to you. You have transformed your energy to project the authentic you and your deepest desires. Finally, you have invoked the Law of Attraction and initiated your magnetic resonance to bring forth your Dream Man. Go out in the world with your new knowledge, trust, and personal power, and keep your eyes and heart open to all possibilities. You've sent out your energetic invitation. You will find each other.

Afterword

My Story of Identity and Authenticity

Writing a book is an incredible journey. You start out with one purpose that you believe is what the book will be about and end up with something quite unexpected. I knew this would be a personal journey for me, but I had no idea it would culminate in the evolution of my own authenticity and become a profound escape from my own paradigm prison. Through this process I have been able to release fear, anger, and even deep-seated hatred that I was unaware was still claiming part of my spirit and my courage.

As a biracial African-American woman growing up in the 1950s to 1960s, I have witnessed and experienced inroads in the advancement of minorities and women over the past fifty years. In the South, where I was born, if you had one drop of African blood you were considered Negro, and not too long ago there were even laws prohibiting blacks from marrying whites. My light-skinned mother and dark-skinned father experienced verbal abuse and discrimination throughout their marriage, but I never sensed any bitterness in either of them. My personal challenges in coming into my own self-esteem and personal power were compounded by my looking Caucasian and being able to pass through doors that dark-skinned African-Americans could not. Part of me felt guilty for escaping the judgment and limitations imposed on blacks, and the other part of me felt shame for being of African-American heritage. As an adult, I had suppressed these feelings of guilt and shame until just recently. Completing this book was the key to opening myself up to unexplored questions. I had to ask myself why I was writing this book. What is my deepest intention and what do I expect to gain? I knew this was a project I was called to do from my heart, with no motivation for fame and wealth, but I had to do a lot of personal exploration to understand my deepest motivation. Now that I'm finished, I have come to realize that I needed to do it for myself, to teach myself what I needed to learn and what I needed to fully embrace about true authenticity and courage to be all that I am.

Until I was nine years old, I didn't give much thought to being of mixed heritage. My parents didn't express judgment or negativity about people and had both black and white friends. Race was something that was rarely mentioned in our home, and after we moved to California, people didn't talk quite so openly about racial differences. Then one day my best friend, Virginia, asked me if I was colored or Spanish. When I asked her why she wanted to know, she told me that her mother didn't want any colored people in her house. My heart dropped to my stomach because her mother was my Brownie leader. Needless to say, I dropped out of Brownies and lost my best friend.

As the years went by, it seemed that more and more incidents happened to prove to me that I was not as good as white people. In 1959, when I was eleven years old, we went to Mississippi to visit my grandmother. It was shocking to me that we had to use drinking fountains and restrooms with signs that read "Colored Only." When we went to the local grocery store owned by a white man my grandparents had known for thirty years, I remember my little sister asking why we had to go in the back door. My heart sank further and there was more proof that I was not equal to whites and not good enough to be accepted. As a teenager, I learned even more about racial lines you just don't cross. At thirteen, I remember an innocent flirtation with a white boy on the school bus turning from playful slaps on the arm into him pushing me down on the ground when we got off the bus and calling me the N-word. With the bus full of kids staring out of the window at me on the ground, I didn't think my heart could sink any further, and the humiliation was devastating. A couple of years later, my best friend Judy told me that I couldn't be John's girlfriend because another white girl liked him, and, as she put it, "You know." Yes, I did know, and it became clear to me that I was different and that was the end of another best friendship.

High school was the first time I didn't go to school on a military base; I was exposed to more black kids there, and saw that they segregated themselves from whites. I was under constant attack from black kids who assumed that I thought I was "better than them" because of my light skin, especially the girls. At school rallies, some of the girls would sit behind me and do loud cheers such as "For the green, for the white, Debby ain't white!" They often taunted me with insults that implied I was pretending to be something I was not, as if they themselves believed being white was better than being black. One day after a rally, a group of black girls circled me and started calling me names, pushing and spitting at me. I was trapped by the group and felt such fear and panic that it nearly caused me to faint. I didn't understand why they hated me when I had never done anything to them. A teacher finally broke it up and sent me to the office. I was in hysterics. When I told them what happened, the principal told me that I must have done or said something to those girls for them to treat me that way. I went home, and I remember staying inside for days, looking out the window, afraid they were going to come to get me and attack me again. I was so afraid to go back to school, and I felt that there was no one who would defend me. The worst part was that the school called my father and told him that the girls had attacked me because I was ashamed of him because he was black. The look on my father's face betrayed his hurt, and it seemed that there was nothing I could say to make him feel better. The truth was that I was ashamed of being black.

As an adult, I didn't realize that the cumulative effect of my childhood experiences, along with some in my adulthood, had been suppressed into hidden anger and hatred for both blacks and whites for not allowing me to have an identity. I belonged nowhere in a world in which people attach themselves to their race, culture, and heritage. There was no group I could connect with, no group that made me feel safe, accepted, respected for who I was as a human being. I remember making a conscious decision at a very young age that I was neither black nor white, and that I would just be me and the best and most perfect person I could be. Inside, however, I separated and isolated myself from others and from my feelings. I chose not to feel anything so that I would never again have to feel the pain of rejection, humiliation, and being less than anyone else. I didn't realize that my unexpressed rage would be converted into self-hatred. It has taken me years of personal growth and spiritual work to trust again, to overcome the fear of having feelings, and to begin to experience real joy and peace in my life.

My father always said, "You have to kill people with kindness." That was his advice for surviving in a culture of discrimination. He also taught me that I need to hold my head high and my shoulders back with pride, to work harder and be smarter, and always leave things better than I found them if I wanted to be successful. And that is what I've done, and it has worked: I've accumulated all the credentials, degrees, and tangible things that represent so-called success in this culture. Money and material things are supposed to give you an identity, social image, happiness, and freedom in life, right? Yet that hasn't been the answer for anyone I know, and it certainly didn't heal my entrenched fear of failure.

Over the past fifty years, laws have changed, and many people have changed their attitudes about equality for women, African Americans, and other minorities. We have seen tremendous progress and achievements in our humanity toward one another. But for many of us there are still the secrets and dark crevices in our hearts that hold pain and memories of our past, and that pain locks us into mental and emotional prisons. These false prisons hold us in old beliefs, patterns, and behaviors that affect our choices, decisions, and the joy and richness of our lives.

This book is not about race, or a soapbox for a resentful victim of our society. It's about authenticity, self-acceptance, and self-love. And it's about honoring who we are and our true power of choice in creating relationships that honor us. What I have just expressed to you in this writing is a kind of "coming out" celebration of myself and all of who I am. My identity does not come from a label of a race, heritage, or skin color. Nor does it come from a man. My identity comes from the full expression of all the aspects of me that are demanding to be known and shown. They're pleading to be freed from the self-imposed suppression of my spirit and calling out for me to be authentic—a real human being. My identity is all of the gifts and experiences I have to share that hopefully can touch others' lives and show a way through their own pain, bringing them the love, joy, and true freedom that I am coming to know. Through writing this book, I have liberated myself from the false prisons of self-denial, fear, anger, and hatred, and unveiled who I am. And my journey continues to evolve.

RELATED READING

Beck, Martha. "Go Tell Alice," part 2 of "The Love List," in *O! magazine*, February 2008.

Dyer, Dr. Wayne. *The Power of Intention—Learning to Co-Create Your World Your Way* (Carlsbad, CA: Hay House, 2004).

Hicks, Esther and Jerry. *The Vortex: Where the Law of Attraction Assembles All Cooperative Relationships* (Carlsbad, CA: Hay House, 2009).

Hinkle, Terry. *Plan Be: The ReMembering, Secrets of the Divine Feminine* (Bloomington, IN: Author House, 2007).

Losier, Michael J. *Law of Attraction: The Science of Attracting More of What You Want and Less of What You Don't* (Victoria, BC: Michael J. Losier, 2006).

Ponder, Catherine. *Open Your Mind to Receive* (Marina del Rey, CA: DeVorss & Company, 1983).

Tolle, Eckhart. *A New Earth: Awakening to your Life's Purpose* (New York: Penguin, 2005).

Tolle, Eckhart. *The Power of Now: A Guide to Spiritual Enlightenment* (Novato, CA: New World Library, 2004).

Zukav, Gary. *The Heart of the Soul: Emotional Awareness* (New York: Fireside, 1989).

APPENDIX A: RELATIONSHIP MODELS

OUTDATED RELATIONSHIP MODEL	EVOLVING RELATIONSHIP MODEL
Qualities: static, limited individual expression, restrictive and highly defined roles and rules, resistance to change, stale, stagnant Role Driven and Survival Based	Qualities: dynamic, expansive individual expression, renewing and re-creating, open to change, adaptable, co-creative, high vitality Choice Driven and Self-Expression Based
BATTLE of the SEXES	**HARMONIOUS RELATIONSHIPS**
Repetitive cycle based on stereotyped roles and behaviors resulting in disillusionment and limited evolution, competition for upper hand, disrupted lives, internal chaos, and loss of joy. Conflict-driven.	Mutually beneficial partnerships that value personal potential and self-expression, marked by compatibility in navigating through ebb and flow of life. Supportive, caring partnerships focused on peace of mind and joy. Cooperation-driven.
ROMANTIC FANTASY/CHEMISTRY ATTRACTION	**ROMANTIC REALITY/ENERGETIC COMPATIBILITY**
• Mate selection is based on temporary, hormonally induced and lust-driven attraction • Stereotypical attraction factors based on image, surface attributes and perceptions • Cultural and media-driven stereotypes of beauty and desirability • Initial passion and lust fuel unsustainable fantasy roles, (i.e. knight in shining armor rescues princess and they live happily "ever after") • Physical appearance (image) and external/surface qualities predetermine standards of compatibility • False assumption that long-term compatibility will automatically follow chemical compatibility. (Divorce statistics prove otherwise) • Female is chosen by male • Male decides and "surprises" female with proposal (often under pressure from her) Results in: Limited available partner choices through hasty judgmental exclusion of candidates; unsustainable relationships.	• Mate selection is primarily based on harmonious feelings and essence compatibility between partners • Lust and chemistry attraction is secondary to long-term compatibility factors • Beauty & desirability defined individually & stereotypes are viewed as caricatures • Reality-based roles and long-term compatibility considerations take priority • Long-term compatibility and energetic resonance takes precedence over external and surface qualities • Energetic compatibility (includes essence, core desires, shared values, complementary lifestyles, and ways of handling conflict, intimacy, and communication) • Coupling/marriage is a mutual decision • Proposal ritual is a formality and celebration Results in: Expanded available partner choices through broader selection criteria based on energetic compatibility; sustainable relationships.

DOMINANT/SUBMISSIVE ROLES	EQUAL PARTNERSHIP
• Tightly defined roles by gender • Masculine dominant / feminine submissive • Masculine superior / feminine inferior • Lack of autonomy and individual identity • Restrictive rules for behavior that define one another and actions viewed as a reflection on each other; one's identity is impacted by the other's behavior • Money equals power only for masculine role; money does not increase submissive role's power • Nurturer/submissive role has no defined monetary value • Masculine primary decision-maker/authority figure • Expectation that each will remain unchanged and value placed on consistent and static routine • Assumption that one needs the other to complete unmet needs and heal wounded self • Parent/Child relationship—Inequality **Results in:** Co-dependency, power struggles/conflict, possessiveness, hostility, deterioration of relationship.	• Shared roles and flexibility in role swapping • Partners hold balanced & equal power roles • Equal value attributed to both feminine and masculine qualities • Individual identity and autonomy • Freedom for individual choices and self-expression; mutual agreement for expectations for each partner role • Money viewed as a shared neutral resource ; does not increase power or define value of provider • Equal value attributed to both provider and nurturer roles; monetary value attributed to nurturer role • Collaborative decision-making; mutual delegation of decisions • Expectation of change/evolution; supporting each other to achieve greatest potential • Self accountability and self-responsibility; one does not complete unmet needs or heal other • Adult/Adult relationship—True equality **Results in:** Mutual support and fulfillment, compatibility, harmony, co-creation.
OUTDATED WAY OF BEING/PERSPECTIVE	EVOLVED WAY OF BEING/PERSPECTIVE
Inauthentic, powerless, fear, resentment, insecurity, cynicism, anger, struggle, violence, externally sought solutions, blame, complaining, alienation, purposeless, boredom, depression, conflicting co-existence, intolerance, resistant to self-awareness, personal growth and change, ensnared in repetitive, negative cycle.	Authentic, self-authority, self-determining, self-worth, self-accountable, empathy, intimacy, belonging, purposeful, adaptable, joyful, optimism, non-judgmental, peaceful co-existence, tolerance, trust in self-discovery process, expansive potential, acceptance of change, flow and positive attraction cycle.

In the above comparison, dominant/masculine is used to refer to the male partner and submissive/feminine refers to female partner. However, dominant and submissive roles can be reversed between male and female and can also apply to same-sex partners resulting in the same dynamics. © 2009 Brilliance MultiMedia

APPENDIX B: MARITAL STATUS

U.S. CENSUS BUREAU Data Set: 2005-2007 American Community; Survey 3-Year Estimates Survey: American Community Survey

Subject	TOTAL	NOW MARRIED (exc separ.)	NOW MARRIED TOTAL	WIDOWED	WIDOWED TOTAL	DIVORCED	DIVORCED TOTAL	SEPARATED	SEPARATED TOTAL	NEVER MARRIED	NEVER MARRIED TOTAL	TOTAL SINGLE
Population 15 yrs & over	237,984,051	50.5%	120,181,946	6.4%	15,230,979	10.5%	24,988,325	2.2%	5,235,649	30.4%	72,347,152	117,802,105
AGE AND SEX												
Males 15 yrs & over	116,033,759	52.6%	61,033,757	2.6%	3,016,878	9.2%	10,675,106	1.9%	2,204,641	33.7%	39,103,377	55,000,002
15 to 19 years	11,027,046	1.1%	121,298	0.2%	22,054	0.1%	11,027	0.1%	11,027	98.6%	10,872,667	10,916,776
20 to 34 years	31,052,854	33.8%	10,495,865	0.1%	31,053	3.8%	1,180,008	1.5%	465,793	60.7%	18,849,082	**20,525,936**
35 to 44 years	21,816,745	63.7%	13,897,267	0.4%	87,267	11.7%	2,552,559	2.7%	589,052	21.4%	4,668,783	7,897,662
45 to 54 years	21,278,749	67.1%	14,278,041	1.1%	234,066	15.7%	3,340,764	2.6%	553,247	13.5%	2,872,631	7,000,708
55 to 64 years	15,208,503	72.6%	11,041,373	2.5%	380,213	15.2%	2,311,692	2.1%	319,379	7.6%	1,155,846	4,167,130
65 years and over	15,649,862	71.5%	11,189,651	14.1%	2,206,631	8.5%	1,330,238	1.3%	203,448	4.5%	704,244	4,444,561
Females 15 yrs & over	121,950,292	48.5%	59,145,892	10.0%	12,195,029	11.6%	14,146,234	2.6%	3,170,708	27.3%	33,292,430	62,804,400
15 to 19 years	10,442,734	2.0%	208,855	0.2%	20,885	0.1%	10,443	0.2%	20,885	97.6%	10,192,108	10,244,322
20 to 34 years	29,779,934	40.8%	12,150,213	0.3%	89,340	5.5%	1,637,896	2.8%	833,838	50.6%	15,068,647	**17,629,721**
35 to 44 years	21,805,589	64.0%	13,955,577	1.1%	239,861	14.4%	3,140,005	4.1%	894,029	16.3%	3,554,311	7,828,206
45 to 54 years	21,954,685	64.0%	14,050,998	3.2%	702,550	18.5%	4,061,617	3.6%	790,369	10.7%	2,349,151	7,903,687
55 to 64 years	16,352,102	62.0%	10,138,303	9.6%	1,569,802	19.2%	3,139,604	2.5%	408,803	6.8%	1,111,943	6,230,151
65 years and over	21,615,248	40.1%	8,667,714	44.3%	9,575,555	10.0%	2,161,525	1.0%	216,152	4.6%	994,301	12,947,534
COMPARISON MALES & FEMALES 35-64 YEARS OLD												
Males- Age 35-64												
35 to 44 years	21,816,745	63.7%	13,897,267	0.4%	87,267	11.7%	2,552,559	2.7%	589,052	21.4%	4,668,783	7,897,662
45 to 54 years	21,278,749	67.1%	14,278,041	1.1%	234,066	15.7%	3,340,764	2.6%	553,247	13.5%	2,872,631	7,000,708
55 to 64 years	15,208,503	72.6%	11,041,373	2.5%	380,213	15.2%	2,311,692	2.1%	319,379	7.6%	1,155,846	4,167,130
Total	58,303,997		39,216,680		701,546		8,205,015		1,461,678		**8,697,261**	19,065,500
Females- Age 35-64												
35 to 44 years	21,805,589	64.0%	13,955,577	1.1%	239,861	14.4%	3,140,005	4.1%	894,029	16.3%	3,554,311	7,828,206
45 to 54 years	21,954,685	64.0%	14,050,998	3.2%	702,550	18.5%	4,061,617	3.6%	790,369	10.7%	2,349,151	7,903,687
55 to 64 years	16,352,102	62.0%	10,138,303	9.6%	1,569,802	19.2%	3,139,604	2.5%	408,803	6.8%	1,111,943	6,230,151
Total	60,112,376		38,144,879		2,512,213		10,341,225		2,093,200		**7,015,405**	21,962,044

Note: Calculation of actual numbers shown above are based on percentages specified in the referenced American Community Survey data.

ACKNOWLEDGMENTS

I wish to give my deepest gratitude to Tamra Fleming, whose incredible and extraordinary talent, intuition, tireless work, and loving support have been immensely instrumental in bringing this work to fruition. I'm deeply grateful to Carrie Morgan, who brought her innate gifts, wisdom, brilliant skills, and enthusiasm to help me expand and enrich the content quality of this book. My deep appreciation goes to Brooke Warner for her expert editing, eloquent contributions, respect for my voice and process, and for always being a valued source of encouragement and knowledge. I want to thank Oriana Green for her outstanding contributions to strengthening and enlivening the content of this book. My special appreciation to Jeanne Gransee Barker's exceptional artistry in bringing such beauty and elegant design to this work. I'm grateful to Robert Stankus for enhancing my message with his creativity and expertise. I am truly grateful to Martina Hoffmann, whose exquisite art has brought beauty and inspiration to this work. My heartfelt thanks to Dr. Bret Lyon, who has been a constant source of guidance, encouragement, and genuine support in bringing my vision to life. My loving thanks to special friends and consultants who have journeyed with me for six years in creating this work: Teryl Jackson, Dr. Cynthia Gallagher, and Diane Rose; and a very special thanks to my good friend Murtis Diallo. I wish to acknowledge my gratitude to Cathy Hawk, Hope Van Vleet, Marie-Rose Phanle, and Ken Iwamura, who have been tremendous teachers and guides in this process. My eternal love and gratitude to my remarkably supportive daughter, Julie Veronese, my stepsons, Nick, Zack, Ben, and Mackenzie Buchta, and my siblings, Jackie Elzig, Shirley Blood, Maxine Boltz, and Ed Garraway. And last, but certainly the best, is the inspiration for *Choose Him*, my wonderful husband Alfred Buchta. He has brought me the magic ingredients of unconditional love and encouragement to pursue all of my dreams and evolve to my highest potential as a woman and human being.

ABOUT THE AUTHOR

© Jamie Grenough Photography

Deb Garraway is the quintessential advocate for authentic feminine potential. Her conviction, life story, and exemplar marriage to her Dream Man reflect her life calling to shift outdated paradigms and help women embrace the belief systems that are at the core of enlightened partnering. *Choose Him* is her wake-up call for women to embody their true selves and attract the Dream Man who values their authenticity and encourages their highest aspirations. *Choose Him* is the first of a series about women's authentic power and potential.

Deb is a contributor to Barbara Stanny's *Breaking Through: Getting Past the Stuck Points in Your Life*, and is an associate producer of Barbara Marx Hubbard's Humanity Ascending series. She also produced *Flocreation*, a CD about the art of living in flow in your own life while supporting others in expressing their brilliance, in 2004.

Deb's decades of gathering women's experiences around their relationships has equipped her with new and creative tools to lead you into the future of your true self and true love. She trained with Clarity International Executive and Leadership Coaching, is a graduate of San Francisco State University, and has an M.B.A. from Pepperdine University. She lives an extraordinarily full life with her husband and four stepsons in Alamo, California.

Being the matchmaker she is, Deb invites you to share your success stories. Girlfriend's gotta know. Visit: www.attractingtheloveofmylife.com: Your comments and suggestions are also appreciated.

www.ingramcontent.com/pod-product-compliance
Lightning Source LLC
Chambersburg PA
CBHW082122230426
43671CB00015B/2777